Divine
Tension *and*
the Mystery
of Balance

SAM BIGGAR

Divine Tension & the Mystery of Balance
Trilogy Christian Publishers
A Wholly Owned Subsidiary of Trinity Broadcasting Network
2442 Michelle Drive
Tustin, CA 92780
Copyright © 2024 by **Sam Biggar**

For information, address Trilogy Christian Publishing
Rights Department, 2442 Michelle Drive, Tustin, CA 92780.
Trilogy Christian Publishing/ TBN and colophon are trademarks of Trinity Broadcasting Network.
For information about special discounts for bulk purchases, please contact Trilogy Christian Publishing.
Trilogy Disclaimer: The views and content expressed in this book are those of the author and may not necessarily reflect the views and doctrine of Trilogy Christian Publishing or the Trinity Broadcasting Network.
10 9 8 7 6 5 4 3 2 1
Library of Congress Cataloging-in-Publication Data is available.
ISBN: 979-8-89041-452-6
ISBN: 979-8-89041-453-3

Endorsements

In Divine Tension and the Mystery of Balance, Sam Biggar delivers fundamental principles that all Christians should have a basic understanding of, but his gift comes in the breakdown of each principle, from the actual translation of the Hebrew and Greek words and the context of the Scripture at the time it was written. The book gives a deeper understanding of God's love and the tension that He uses to bring us into greater accord with Himself. The book is a great resource and could be used as a Bible study for small groups. I hope the book enlightens, renews, and gives people a greater trust that God is who He says He is, He does what He says He will do, and He loves you beyond measure.

Dr. Robin Deremer

As a follower of Jesus, I have wrestled to find a harmony with parts of the Bible that seem to disagree. Sam Biggar's Divine Tension and the Mystery of Balance not only brought clarity to complicated biblical concepts, but it also helped me to incorporate them into my spiritual life. I have accepted that my journey with Jesus must be in the perfect balance and tension of His truth and love.

Pastor David Moynihan

Introduction

Please read this first!

Most people, if they are like me, skip the introduction. I want to get to the meat of the book, and the introductions always seems like such a waste of time. When you write a book, the introduction takes on a new dimension. You want to tell people why you wrote the book before they read it. It gives context to the writing. The issues in this book are complex and often misunderstood. One of the things that I have learned is that WE MAKE THEM COMPLEX! They are very simple to the Lord God. Jehovah has all the answers we need if we would seek Him and TRUST what He tells us. Having said that, I want the reader to know that I certainly do not have all the answers. But what I can tell you about these subjects is what the Lord has taught me. However, the wisdom of God is like a great mountain, what we see at the bottom is not what we see from the pinnacle. Please understand - if you do not read what you expect, or my understanding varies from your own, please read on with an open mind, and you may just be blessed for doing so.

There are a great many things that puzzle us today. We think that we are intelligent enough to figure everything out. Those who do not believe in God, or even a 'first cause,' believe that quantum physics and 'string theory' will eventually lead to the 'reason for everything.' Scientists now have a theory, based on the String Theory, that we no longer live in a universe but a multiverse. Multiple universes, multiplied dimensions and more and more theories, based on other theories, which are presented as fact. It seems to me that looking at history over the last two hundred years, with the advancement of science and knowledge, we should conclude that things will change about what we believe to be true the deeper we understand the things that are, or exist now. We were convinced that Pluto was a planet for years, now it is just a big space rock. A website I looked at recently gave eight 'scientific' facts that have changed over the years. Things like this should not surprise us since we don't have all the information, and what we do have is so often misinterpreted. The Apostle Paul said that 'we see through a glass darkly.' Now we create particle colliders to attempt to understand how everything began not knowing what will happen if we push the envelope too far and possibly ignite the atmosphere that sustains life here on Earth. (Just kidding, but maybe??) Is it possible that there are mysteries which we will never solve? Does that then mean that we stop trying? I believe that God made us curious for a reason. We strive to figure things out, to solve problems and gain understanding. I believe that the mysteries of the universe are there for the solving, and we are drawn to solve them. Proverbs 25:2, NASB, says, *"It is the glory of God to conceal a matter, But the glory of kings is to search out a matter."* I believe that God wants us to seek wisdom and understanding. When we do I think

He knows that it will inevitably lead to Him.

There is a struggle that I have seen in trying to solve these mysteries over the years. Not surprisingly, knowing human nature, we end up at different ends of the spectrum on some of these issues, especially if they are Scriptural issues. I have seen, too often, that the tension that God created to hold some of these things in balance is thrown out, and we end up on one side or the other. From that chosen side we build a doctrinal stronghold which we are then obligated to defend, and someone else feels obligated to knock down. What I have discovered is what I want to share with you in this book. I believe that God created a tension in the universe that holds things in balance - much like a tight rope. When the opposite ends are secure, the rope is tought. We can traverse the chasm (subject) if we know how to keep our balance. If the rope is too loose, we will not be able to keep our balance, and we will fall. This tension, I believe, is what is seen in the reason why an atom does not fly apart when two like polarized particles are in its nucleus. Like charges usually repel, yet the atom stays together in what scientists call the strong attraction or strong force.

"The strong force was first proposed to explain why atomic nuclei do not fly apart. It seemed that they would do so due to the repulsive electromagnetic force between the positively charged protons located in the nucleus. It was later found that the strong force not only holds nuclei together, but is also responsible for binding together the quarks that make up hadrons. Strong force interactions are important in ... holding hadrons together," according to "The Four Forces" physics course material from Duke University. "The fundamental strong interaction holds the constituent quarks of a hadron together, and the residual force holds hadrons together with each other, such as the proton and neutrons in a nucleus." (1)

Of course, I believe that this attraction, force, and tension are all created by God. At the risk of getting too scientific, the illustration of the tight rope seems to fit nicely with what God has planned to keep the universe in balance. This balance applies to other aspects of creation that we debate as theological issues. Some of these things are laws that govern our universe, and some are ideas or realities that are in balance because that is how God designed and built the universe. I will exam some of these issues one by one in this book. My hope is that you will be enlightened by this material and even stirred up spiritually to dig deeper for yourself. Remember, "It is the glory of kings (mankind) to search out a matter." It is also important for me to give these doctrines a 'human' element. God does not live, most often, in the lofty halls of academia, but rather in the trenches of humanity where His love and grace matter most. I remember going to a Christian day school in a poverty-stricken part of a 'third world country.' There were approximately thirty to forty students per classroom. The desks were pushed together so that you would have had to climb over the front desks to get the back desks.

The children went to school from approximately 6:00 a.m. to 6:00 p.m. They had old car tires as their toys. After we toured the school, the principal gathered the students to sing for our group. There were around four hundred children who came out and lined up to sing for us. I was moved with compassion because many had tattered and worn uniforms to wear. I was even more moved when I heard the sincerity and pureness in them as they sang to us. Even as I write this, my eyes well up because I remember so vividly being there and hearing them. I wanted to go out and buy them all new uniforms and raise money so they had proper toys to play with during recess. But the Holy Spirit reminded me that if those things happened, they would be like our own children who have more than enough, and they would lose the sincerity and love for God knowing that He was their everything and not a uniform they may wear or toys they may play with at recess. I saw up close and personal that God really lived in the trenches, and His love and grace was so evident there. Consequently, I had to ask myself what the doctrinal issues in this book would mean to those kids, and would they care? What I arrived at is that these issues are important, but mostly because they tell the story of our amazing God. They tell us who He is and how He loves us. They help us to clearly see that God is supremely worthy of our trust if for no other reason than the lengths He went to so that we could be in communion with Him.

What I have also discovered is that there are many things that have a tension and balance in life. These things are more than just Scriptural issues - although Scripture speaks to a great variety of issues if we are willing to search them out. Many of these understood concepts are at the forefront of much in current culture. In a time when everything that has been believed and taught is being questioned, there needs to be a return to a Scriptural and Godly foundation. Proverbs 9:10 reads, *'The fear of the Lord is the beginning of wisdom, and the knowledge of the Holy One is understanding.'* If we are a few degrees off this mark at the beginning, where will we then finally end up? Also of note is, that one of the definitions of balance is, 'A state of equilibrium between contrasting, opposing or interacting elements.' Read on, and hopefully, you can find equilibrium.

All Scripture comes from the from the New American Standard Bible unless otherwise noted.

Table of Contents

CHAPTER ONE

What are All These Things? And Where is the Balance?

When we think about balance we can see it in the illustration of a seesaw on the playground, or even an old scale - before the ones that showed the weight as a digital read out. For a seesaw to work properly there needs to be a balance. The same is true for a set of scales. Years ago, you would have to put a, let's say, one pound weight on one side of a scale and then put the product on the other side until the scale was balanced. Then you would know that you had a pound of product such as salt, food, or whatever. Having a balanced scale was what you wanted.

There are many things that are opposites of which we may understand there is a need for balance, but some opposites are not as important as others. Like soft and hard. They are opposites. Some people like hard candy and some like soft candy. Others may like both or may have a preference in the moment. Not many people want to eat hard bread that came out of the bag and not the toaster. Some things need a balance, and thankfully, God, has balanced some things in the world. Some things He wants our cooperation to find balance. Our world has a balance of hot and cold. There is a reason for the polar ice caps and the cold at the north and south poles. There is also a reason for the warmth at the equator. God created all these things perfectly balanced. He created hot and cold to bring and sustain life on earth. This could be a different and longer chapter to lay out the balance of hot and cold in the earth. Think weather, and that would be a starting point of the balance of hot and cold on our planet.

Here is list of some opposites. With some, balance is important, with others not so much.

Hot and Cold	Hero and Villain	Apathy and Empathy
Light and Dark	Courage and Fear	End and Beginning
Soft and Hard	Anguish and Joy	Love and Hate
Slow and Fast	Left and Right	Always and Never
Shy and Bold	Anxious and Calm	Truth and Lie
Skinny and ... not Skinny	Silence and Sound	Dead and Alive
Short and Tall	Shallow and Deep	Advantage and Disadvantage
Good and Bad	Strong and Weak	Give and Take

This website has a complete list. https://7esl.com/opposites/#OppositesAntonyms_A

Why do we need to find a balance between soft and hard? We may not even think about a balance between soft and hard. We may not think that there is a balance necessary. However, when we really think about opposites, we may find that there are some instances where a balance is important. Here is a Scripture to consider with soft and hard.

A soft answer turns away wrath: Proverbs 15:1a, NKJV. Understanding this verse, what would the opposite do? *But a harsh (hard) word stirs up anger.* Proverbs 15:1b. Do we want to add fuel to a fire, or would it be wise and bring balance to add water by our response? Here is another Scripture about hard.

Many therefore of his disciples, when they had heard this, said, this is an hard saying; who can hear it? John 6:60. This was the response of Jesus's disciples not the crowd. Their action after Jesus taught them that He was the Bread from Heaven: *From that time many of his disciples went back and walked no more with him.* John 6:66. Was a hard word needed to distinguish the wheat from the tares? You can decide for yourself. Again, we *can* find a balance between soft and hard.

LIGHT AND DARK

This is a subject where we need to seek to understand so we can find a balance. Light is something created by God. Scientifically, there is no such thing as darkness. Darkness is simply the absence of light. There is, however, a difference between spiritual light and physical light. We experience physical light in the physical world every day.

We see the sunrise and the sunset. There is day and there is night. We desire things to be lit when the sun sets so we have candles, lightbulbs, flashlights, and streetlights. All of these are physical lights. In the physical realm, which is the creation of the Lord God Almighty, there is a balance of physical light. We may add other sources of physical light to help balance the spiritual darkness in the world. As an example, we add streetlights to dissuade criminals from criminal activity. This type of activity is dark spiritually and is energized by spiritual darkness. *For we wrestle not against flesh and blood, but against principalities, against powers, against the rulers of the darkness of this world, against spiritual wickedness in high places.* Ephesians 6:12. Our physical light that we add to dissuade both physical and spiritual darkness does not diminish that spiritual darkness. We can have an effect, like driving back the darkness, but only God Himself can extinguish spiritual darkness. **Because God is light**… *This then is the message which we have heard of him, and declare unto you, that God is light, and in him is no darkness at all.* 1 John 1:5, **and He is Spirit,** … *God is spirit, and those who worship Him must worship in spirit and truth."* John 4:24, **then He is spiritual light only.** There is no darkness in God as the verse above states. So, the opposite of God's spiritual lightness is spiritual darkness.

Though it may be difficult to understand how spiritual darkness was allowed to happen, we do know that the origin of all spiritual darkness is Lucifer. Isaiah 14 and

Ezekiel 28 give us a clear indication that this was the origin of spiritual darkness. The Hebrew word translated Lucifer is hêylêl, hay-lale'; from H1984 (in the sense of brightness); the morning-star. Lucifer actually is derived from the meaning of the Hebrew word as it is translated into Latin. As believers we need to recognize that there is dark spiritual activity all around us and not be quick to point the finger at what we see with our eyes and hear with our ears. We need to be like Jesus, (...*And He [Jesus] will delight in the fear of the Lord, And He will not judge by what His eyes see, nor make a decision by what His ears hear; But with righteousness He will judge the poor, And decide with fairness for the afflicted of the earth;* Isaiah 11:3-4), and judge by what God says and not what we see and hear. Jesus also said, *Jesus answered and was saying to them, "Truly, truly, I say to you, the Son can do nothing of Himself, unless it is something He sees the Father doing; for whatever the Father does, these things the Son also does in like manner. For the Father loves the Son, and shows Him all things that He Himself is doing;* John 5:19-20. This indicates that Jesus was connected spiritually with the Father and listened to His Father's spiritual guidance. This is how we balance light and darkness. We do not have the full capacity to understand completely spiritual lightness and darkness. Since this is true, then we must rely on the wisdom and discernment of the Holy Spirit, and we must listen to the voice of Jesus directing us. *My sheep hear My voice, and I know them, and they follow Me;* John 10:27. We can become discerning ourselves, but if Jesus relied on and trusted His Father this is a clear indication that we should also when it comes to discerning light and dark. *But solid food is for the mature, who because of practice have their senses trained to discern good and evil.* Hebrews 5:14. John Paul Jackson has a clear presentation of the lightness and darkness in his teaching called, *True Spirituality.* It is well worth the cost and time to listen to his presentation. (2)

COURAGE AND FEAR. THE TENSION BETWEEN FEAR AND FAITH.

Mark Twain said, "Courage is resistance to fear, mastery of fear, not absence of fear." God says, *5 No one will be able to stand against you all the days of your life. As I was with Moses, so I will be with you; I will never leave you nor forsake you. 6 Be strong and courageous, because you will lead these people to inherit the land, I swore to their ancestors to give them. 7 "Be strong and very courageous. Be careful to obey all the law my servant Moses gave you; do not turn from it to the right or to the left, that you may be successful wherever you go. 8 Keep this Book of the Law always on your lips; meditate on it day and night, so that you may be careful to do everything written in it. Then you will be prosperous and successful. 9 Have I not commanded you? Be strong and courageous. Do not be afraid; do not be discouraged, for the Lord your God will be with you wherever you go."* Joshua 1:5-9. Mark Twain was raised in Christianity, but he later rejected his orthodox upbringing. His quote is good, but what is the foundation upon which he stands? Is it soul power? Reading the passage in Joshua, the foundation for courage for the believer, is trust in God. When we know what God is doing then it is easy to trust in His providential care for us. If we believe in His sovereignty..., why do we need to be afraid? If we believe that He is with us and for us... what is there to fear? So, where is the balance between courage and fear, and how do we get to that balance? If you read some of the secular sources, there are many ways to cope with fears and even face fear. Some of this is good strategy, and it can be helpful. What is missing is the spiritual element and the deeper reliance upon God.

11 Now the heart of the king of Aram was enraged over this thing; and he called his servants and said to them, "Will you tell me which of us is for the king of Israel?" 12 One of his servants said, "No, my lord, O king; but Elisha, the prophet who is in Israel, tells the king of Israel the words that you speak in your bedroom." 13 So he said, "Go and see where he is, that I may send and take him." And it was told him, saying, "Behold, he is in Dothan." 14 He sent horses and chariots and a great army there, and they came by night and surrounded the city. 15 Now when the attendant of the man of God had risen early and gone out, behold, an army with horses and chariots was circling the city. And his servant said to him, "Alas, my master! What shall we do?" 16 So he answered, "Do not fear, for those who are with us are more than those who are with them." 17 Then

Elisha prayed and said, "O Lord, I pray, open his eyes that he may see." And the Lord opened the servant's eyes and he saw; *and behold, the mountain was full of horses and chariots of fire all around Elisha.* 2 Kings 6:11-17. This is an interesting passage because the servant of Elisha was in fear. Elisha's response is poignant and amazing from a non-spiritual point of view. Surely his servant was about to tell him that he was crazy and what was he talking about. Before he had a chance to ask what he was talking about and make any statements, his eyes were opened, and now he realized that there was no reason to fear. He now had a different sense of who God was and a look into the spirit realm. This reality about the power of God can be true for us because John said, *4 You are from God, little children, and have overcome them; because greater is He who is in you than he who is in the world.* 1 John 4:4. Do we believe that this is true for us? Or maybe a better question would be, do we believe in God, or do we believe God? Is God a liar? Or does He tell the truth? If we really believe that God never lies and always tells the truth, then all of our fears boil down to whether or not we - believe God - whether or not we believe in who He is and so believe what He says.

Many people, even believers, say that they believe in God, but if we truly believed Him, we would live differently. We would live in faith, not fear, and we would have a Spirit - charged courage that Paul told Timothy about when he said, *5 For I am mindful of the sincere faith within you, which first dwelt in your grandmother Lois and your mother*

Eunice, and I am sure that it is in you as well. 6 For this reason I remind you to kindle afresh the gift of God which is in you through the laying on of my hands. 7 For God has not given us a spirit of timidity, but of power and love and discipline. 2 Timothy 1:5-7. This is the NASB version of this passage. The KJV is usually quoted which says, *For God has not given us a spirit of fear, but of power and of love and of a sound mind.* The Greek word for fear in this verse is not phobia, but is: δειλία deilía, di-lee'-ah; timidity: - fear. This word means timidity, fearfulness, cowardice. The other Greek word for fear, phobia is: φοβέω phobéō, fob-eh'-o; and means: to frighten, i.e., (passively) to be alarmed; by analogy, to be in awe of, i.e., revere: —be (+ sore) afraid, fear (exceedingly), reverence. We often think of this fear as bad since our culture has so many phobias, but the other Greek word deilla is really the wrong kind of fear, as you can read, phobia has a reverential awe included in why there is fear. So, when other believers tell us that God has not given us a spirit of fear, they are dead on that God does not want us to fear or be cowardly. Rather, He has given us the Holy Spirit of 'power, love and a sound (or disciplined) mind.'

Years ago, one of my spiritual mentors was sitting down to lunch with my wife, Lori, and me. During the meal he paused and looked at me and said that I was the only person he had ever met who had no fear. I was blessed by his recognition that I had no fears. I have chosen over the years to address any fear and challenge that fear by faith.

I choose to walk in faith and not to walk in fear. John Paul Jackson said, "What you fear you empower... so fear God!" This fear of God is described by the Greek word phobia, a reverential awe of God. If you meet someone who does not fear God, it is because they have never met God. Anyone who has truly met God, in any way, has a reverential awe and fear because of who He is as God. This is why He says 'I Am who I Am.' Faith is the opposite of fear. The story of Joshua, in chapter one of Joshua, is a good example of why faith trumps fear.

2 Now then, you and all these people, get ready to cross the Jordan River into the land I am about to give to them— to the Israelites. 3 I will give you every place where you set your foot, as I promised Moses. 4 Your territory will extend from the desert to Lebanon, and from the great river, the Euphrates—all the Hittite country—to the Mediterranean Sea in the west. 5 No one will be able to stand against you all the days of your life. As I was with Moses, so I will be with you; I will never leave you nor forsake you. 6 Be strong and courageous, because you will lead these people to inherit the land I swore to their ancestors to give them. 7 "Be strong and very courageous. Be careful to obey all the law my servant Moses gave you; do not turn from it to the right or to the left, that you may be successful wherever you go. 8 Keep this Book of the Law always on your lips; meditate on it day and night, so that you may be careful to do everything written in it. Then you will be prosperous and successful. 9 Have I not commanded you? Be strong and courageous. Do not be afraid; do not be discouraged, for the Lord your God will be with you wherever you go." Joshua 1:3-9.

God tells Joshua that He will be with him. But even before that He tells Joshua that He will give him every place he sets his foot. Just the promises in this short passage would be enough for me to be 'strong and courageous.' Look at what God promised Joshua and think, would you be afraid, or would you be able to walk in faith into the promise land knowing the war to get there? I love that phrase, "Have I not commanded you?" This command is like a five-star general telling a colonel that he has given him a mission and commanded him to complete it. With that mission comes all the resources that the colonel will need to be successful. This is even better though because God tells Joshua as the Lord of heaven and earth that He..., *'so I will be with thee: I will not fail thee, nor forsake thee.'* (KJV). Imagine God saying that He will not *fail* us. Joshua had a part to fulfill, obey the Law, meditate on the Law, and he would be successful. God always works in us and through us when we abide in Him like Jesus said in John 15.

Understanding all that has just been laid out we can see why there is no reason to be afraid. We should also be able to see how we can walk in faith with God Almighty.

When we go back to the beginning of the chapter and look at the 'opposites' listed, we should be challenged to figure out some of the Scriptural balances for these opposites on our own. What does Scripture have to say about good and bad or evil? Is there a balance between good and evil? When we look at the teaching of Scripture and put together our own research, then the reality of God in these various things is evident and impactful to us. Therefore, the rest of the opposites listed will not all be discussed, but we will leave room for your own study.

CHAPTER TWO

Sovereignty and Freewill: The Balance of Creator and Created

What does it mean for God to be sovereign? This question has been debated by theologians for millennium. Most theologians that hold to a historical, traditional, fundamental view believe that God is absolutely Sovereign over all that He has created. Psalms 33:11, - *'The counsel of the LORD stands forever, the plans of His heart from generation to generation.'* Proverbs 19:21, - *'Many plans are in a man's heart, but the counsel of the LORD will stand.'* Ephesians 1:11, - *'... also we have obtained an inheritance, having been predestined according to His purpose who works all things after the counsel of His will...'*

The philosophers of old and then down through the passage of time, from Democritus and Leucippus, in the fifth century BC to John Searle in our current time, have all sought to understand and even explain free will. Searle wrote in 2007, "The persistence of the free will problem in philosophy seems to me something of a scandal. After all these centuries of writing about free will, it does not seem to me that we have made very much progress." (3) This is a good summary of all the back and forth of philosophers, thinkers, writers, and theologians about free will and sovereignty.

Before the debate was a major theological one, even ancient philosophers tried to understand 'determinism' and free will. Determinism is the thought that all that has happened is determined, and that there is causality for all that takes place in the universe. Human will is only free in that the choices are determined. This sounds like an illusion of free will rather than free will in actuality. If pure determinism exists, then what is the answer to moral responsibility on the part of sentient beings like humans?

What is interesting and noted by some philosophers, is that ancient theological writers don't argue about sovereignty and free will. It is only the secular thinkers who take up the debate, and with the westernization of the church in 325AD, the church theologians begin to debate the issue as well. There are different views on the subject throughout the history of the church. Most writers seek to sway readers to choose one side or the other. Either God is sovereign, or man has a free will. Sam Storms lays out the historical, traditional, fundamental view with correlating Scripture in his article, "Ten Things You Should Know About the Sovereignty of God." (https://www.crosswalk.com/faith/bible-study/10-things-you-should-know-about-the-sovereignty-of-god.html). However, this is not the only side of the debate.

The beginnings of the theological debate surely happened before Paul's great treaties on the matter in Romans 9. Surely this debate started when people began to reason after there was some concrete revelation about Jehovah, the God of Abraham, Isaac, and Jacob. Surely Job must have had some questions regarding sovereignty when he was going through his trial of faith. Though he never blames God, and in fact recognizes His goodness later, during the most severe part of the trial, he questions God about the why of his suffering. He holds on to his integrity that he has not sinned despite his 'friends' trying to convince him otherwise that he has sinned. When God does show up in all His majesty only then does Job truly recognize His sovereignty. Though this is the writer's opinion, like stated before, ancient theological writers seem to fall into a non-debate position like the Apostle Paul.

Paul takes up the question of free will and sovereignty in Romans 9, but there is an interesting conclusion to the question about which is true, and which is not true. When Paul describes, very plainly, that God is sovereign and can do as He pleases, Paul anticipates the most logical question to follow that statement, *"You will say to me then, "Why does He still find fault? For who resists His will?"* (Verse 19). This is where Paul could have ended the debate once and for all, yet he never answers the question. He only poses a question of his own. We are left wondering if Paul's question is because we understand the answer already, and so Paul never answers the question, or if we are somehow left to figure it out on our own.

However, years later, Augustine takes up the debate, arguing the point of free will and the issue of sin in the early 5th century AD. Augustine writes about sovereignty and free will in connection to the sin of mankind from a philosophical perspective. He argues from a perspective of reasoning through the implications of the Scriptures and the doctrines that proceed from the Scriptures. When he uses Scripture, he applies reasoning and argues through to the conclusions he presents. Down through the centuries, there have been others who have debated this issue. There is a good, concise paper on the history of this debate at: https://www.informationphilosopher.com/freedom/history/. Check it out, it is worth reading.

Being too simplistic leaves the theologians to say that the issue is not completely covered, so how can one draw conclusions? On the other hand, there could be endless debates about subjects like total depravity, and these leave the average reader behind, unwilling to finish the book.

Having said all that, history is important in any debate. It gives context, and conclusions can be drawn based on the writing and teaching of others. The purpose of this book is not a history lesson, but to lay some groundwork and move into the Scriptural viewpoint of each side - like the two sides of a tightrope. The first question that needs to be answered or described from Scripture is whether mankind has a free will. The verses for free will are listed - followed by a brief commentary and then an overall conclusion.

VERSES ABOUT FREE WILL: THERE ARE MANY MORE, BUT THIS IS A GOOD SAMPLING:

Psalms 54:6 - *Willingly I will sacrifice to You; I will give thanks to Your name, O Lord, for it is good.*

Psalms 119:108 - *O accept the freewill offerings of my mouth, O Lord, And teach me Your ordinances.*

Leviticus 22:23 - *In respect to an ox or a lamb which has an overgrown or stunted member, you may present it for a freewill offering, but for a vow it will not be accepted.*

Psalms 31:4 - *You will pull me out of the net which they have secretly laid for me, For You are my strength.*

Philippians 2:13 - *For it is God who is at work in you, both to will and to work for His good pleasure.*

Romans 8:21- *That the creation itself also will be set free from its slavery to corruption into the freedom of the glory of the children of God.*

Galatians 5:13 - *For you were called to freedom, brethren; only do not turn your freedom into an opportunity for the flesh, but through love serve one another.*

Leviticus 7:16 - *But if the sacrifice of his offering is a votive or a freewill offering, it shall be eaten on the day that he offers his sacrifice, and on the next day what is left of it may be eaten.*

Ezra 7:13 - *I have issued a decree that any of the people of Israel and their priests and the Levites in my kingdom who are willing to go to Jerusalem, may go with you.*

John 8:36 - *So if the Son makes you free, you will be free indeed.*

2 Chronicles 31:14 - *Kore, the son of Imnah the Levite, the keeper of the Eastern Gate, was over the freewill offerings of God, to apportion the contributions for the Lord and the most holy things.*

Romans 6:18 - *And having been freed from sin, you became slaves of righteousness.*

Ezra 8:28 - *Then I said to them, "You are holy to the Lord, and the utensils are holy; and the silver and the gold are a freewill offering to the Lord God of your fathers."*

Ephesians 6:8 - *Knowing that whatever good thing each one does, this he will receive back from the Lord, whether slave or free.*

Philemon 1:14 - *But without your consent I did not want to do anything, so that your goodness would not be, in effect, by compulsion, but of your own free will.*

John 8:32 - *And you will know the truth, and the truth will make you free.*

After reading these verses, we can draw the conclusion, based on these Scriptures, that humanity possesses a free will. But these are not the only things that we have to determine that we have a free will. We know this by experience. We know that we have a choice between right and wrong, good and evil. We are faced with choices every day. Some of those choices are serious when we choose between right and wrong. We know what is right even if we deny that there is a God. Should we lie? No, but do we? Sometimes we resist the urge to lie and tell the truth even to our own detriment. We can also see the the struggle in those around us. We watch our children struggle between good and evil, right and wrong. We even know when they are lying, and we are blessed when they tell the truth. Therefore, the only conclusion is that humanity has a free will.

VERSES ABOUT SOVEREIGNTY:

Ephesians 1:11 - *In him we have obtained an inheritance, having been predestined according to the purpose of him who works all things according* to the counsel of his will...

Romans 8:28 - *And we know that for those who love God all things work together for good, for those who are called according to his purpose...*

Colossians 1:16–17 - *For by him all things were created, in heaven and on earth, visible and invisible, whether thrones or dominions or rulers or authorities—all things were created through him and for him. And he is before all things, and in him all things hold together.*

Isaiah 45:7–9 - *I form light and create darkness; I make well-being and create calamity; I am the LORD, who does all these things. "Shower, O heavens, from above, and let the clouds rain down righteousness; let the earth open, that salvation and righteousness may bear fruit; let the earth cause them both to sprout; I the LORD have created it. Woe to him who strives with him who formed him, a pot among earthen pots! Does the clay say to him who forms it, 'What are you making?' or 'Your work has no handles?'*

Proverbs 16:33 - *The lot is cast into the lap, but it's every decision is from the LORD.*

Job 42:2 - *I know that you can do all things, and that no purpose of yours can be thwarted.*

Acts 4:27–28 - *For truly in this city there were gathered together against your holy servant Jesus, whom you anointed, both Herod and Pontius Pilate, along with the Gentiles and the peoples of Israel, to do whatever your hand and your plan had predestined to take place.*

Ephesians 1:4-6 - *For he chose us in him before the creation of the world to be holy and blameless in his sight. In love he predestined us for adoption to sonship through Jesus Christ, in accordance with his pleasure and will— to the praise of his glorious grace, which he has freely given us in the One he loves.*

Proverbs 19:21 - *Many are the plans in a person's heart, but it is the Lord's purpose that prevails.*

Isaiah 43:13 - *Even from eternity I am He, And there is none who can deliver out of My hand; I act and who can reverse it?*

Romans 9: 16-20 - *It does not, therefore, depend on human desire or effort, but on God's mercy. For Scripture says to Pharaoh: "I raised you up for this very purpose, that I might display my power in you and that my name might be proclaimed in all the earth. "Therefore, God has mercy on whom he wants to have mercy, and he hardens whom he wants to harden. One of you will say to me: "Then why does God still blame us? For who is able to resist his will?" But who are you, a human being, to talk back to God?*

Again, these are not all the verses about sovereignty, but these verses seem to have more of a declaration about the sovereignty of God than the verses about man's free will. We can say, based on these Scriptures, that God is sovereign over the creation and the things that happen in creation. One other interesting thought about sovereignty is the death of Jesus. Scripture has over three hundred prophecies about Jesus. Prophecies that are about His life and His death. The fulfillment of these verses is declarative proof of the sovereignty of God. Satan knew these verses long before Jesus was born, yet he could not subvert the will and plans of God. Therefore, the obvious conclusion is that Jehovah God is sovereign over all creation.

So then what is the conclusion of this matter? Both sides have many verses which are used in the debate as 'proof texts' for their position. Also, both sides have books that explain the proof texts of the opposite side. The free will camp explains the sovereignty verses and why they really are not talking about sovereignty the way the sovereignty camps say these verses talk about sovereignty. The sovereignty camp does the same thing only in reverse. So, what is to be done, and what is to be concluded when both camps have so much Scriptural basis for their belief? The conclusion that seems most plausible is - both are true. It is not either-or, but both-and. This is the mystery of balance in these two great doctrines, and the Divine tension that allows us to walk the tightrope. What I believe is that these two great truths, which seem so contradictory to us, are clear in the mind of God.

These two truths fit together and make sense in the infinite mind of Jehovah God even if in our limited intelligence they do not fit together for us. There are some things in the world that have been postulated by people of genius that may not make complete sense to us. Einstein's $E=mc^2$ may be one of those postulations. We may not understand how to measure the amount of energy stored in a glass of water using the $E=mc^2$ formula, but that does not make it less true if we do understand and could turn the water into energy. We may not even understand all the ramification of $E=mc^2$ mostly because we do not have the mental capacity of an Einstein or some other genius in the world. So, if we accept that there are greater minds than ours that may understand $E=mc^2$ more than we do, why would we not accept that free will and sovereignty are understood by the infinite mind of our God, and there is a balance between these two seemingly opposing concepts?

Can we lose our salvation? Maybe I should not dive into this debate, but it has a tie into sovereignty and free will. Here, in this debate, if you follow my previous conclusion that both are true, then where does that leave the answer to this question? What is the balance on this issue if there is a divine tension that brings balance to free will and sovereignty? Yes, God is sovereign, and yes, man has a free will, but where do they come together in the question of salvation? There are many verses again, that point to whichever side you choose to be on in this debate. Many fear that if we don't preach a 'lose your salvation' message then those who are saved will surely fall away into a fire-filled eternity. Those who preach eternal security sometimes see that security as a net to catch us when we sin, but there is always a return to God for those who are truly born again. Since there are many verses on both sides, and therefore is reason to stand on either side, I will conclude this short debate with a Scripture that speaks of both sides and may be a clue as to the answer.

John 1:12-13 - *But as many as received Him, to them He gave the right to become children of God, even to those who believe in His name, who were born, not of blood nor of the will of the flesh nor of the will of man, but of God.*

Believers are born again not of our own will, but of God's will.

CHAPTER THREE

The Hypostatic Union: The Balance of Divinity and Humanity

The term, hypostatic union, is a theological term. One definition is: 'Hypostatic union is a technical term in Christian theology employed in mainstream Christology to describe the union of Christ's humanity and divinity in one hypostasis, or individual existence. The most basic explanation for the hypostatic union is Jesus Christ being both fully God and fully man.' (6) So how is this possible, and why are we writing about it here? We read in the Scriptures that 'all things are possible with God.' The context of this verse is about faith, but it has a wider application to everything. God has all power and can do things that we can only dream of as humans. The reason for writing about it here is that there is a balance in the hypostatic union that only God can have. We need to understand as much as we can and how it works so that we stand in faith on the Word of God. Though there may be some mystery here, there are some things that we do know. Another intent for all that is written here may not necessarily be to present a position, but so the reader searches deeper for themselves and reaches their own conclusion. Searching deeper does not only mean the Scriptures, but God Himself. We must be concerned to know the writer of the Scriptures as well as we do the Scriptures.

NICENE CREED (AD 325)

We believe in one God, the Father Almighty, Maker of all things visible and invisible. And in one Lord Jesus Christ , the Son of God, begotten of the Father [the only-begotten; that is, of the essence of the Father, God of God], Light of Light, very God of very God, begotten, not made, being of one substance (homoousion) with the Father; by whom all things were made [both in heaven and on earth]; who for us men, and for our salvation, came down and was incarnate and was made man; he suffered, and the third day he rose again, ascended into heaven; from thence he shall come to judge the quick and the dead.

CHALCEDONIAN DEFINITION OF THE HYPOSTATIC UNION (AD 451)

Therefore, following the holy fathers, we all with one accord teach men to acknowledge one and the same Son, our Lord Jesus Christ, at once complete in Godhead and complete in manhood, truly God and truly man, consisting also of a reasonable soul and body; of one substance with the Father as regards his Godhead, and at the same time of one substance with us as regards his manhood; like us in all respects, apart from sin; as regards his Godhead, begotten of the Father before the ages, but yet as regards his manhood begotten, for us men and for our salvation, of Mary the Virgin, the God-bearer; one and the same Christ, Son, Lord, Only-begotten, recognized in two natures, without confusion, without change, without division, without separation; the distinction of nature's being in no way annulled by the union, but rather the characteristics of each nature being preserved and coming together to form one person and subsistence, not as parted or separated into two persons, but one and the same Son and Only-begotten God the Word, Lord Jesus Christ; even as the prophets from earliest times spoke of him, and our Lord Jesus Christ himself taught us, and the creed of the fathers has handed down to us.

These two creeds of the faith are here so that there is context to this issue and understanding of the position on the hypotactic union by the early church.

The foundation of the hypostatic union is the birth of Jesus. The main Scripture is John's Gospel chapter one, verses 1-4; 14.

In the beginning was the Word, and the Word was with God, and the Word was God. He was in the beginning with God. All things came into being through Him, and apart from Him nothing came into being that has come into being. In Him was life, and the life was the Light of men.

14 The Word became flesh and made his dwelling among us. We have seen his glory, the glory of the one and only Son, who came from the Father, full of grace and truth.

There is speculation around the virgin birth, such as, why was it a virgin birth? Some have said that it is because the sin nature is transmitted through the father, so Jesus could not have a human father. Some say that with Jesus specifically there was a curse on the Davidic line of Joseph so that no one from the descendants of Jeconiah's line could sit on the throne of David. (Jeremiah 22). This is why, the argument goes, that Mary was also a direct descendant of David giving Jesus the kingly succession. These are speculations with some biblical evidence, but is the truth just something simple like Jesus was to be a first-born son? As a side bar with an interesting thought direction in Godly thinking, who was Jacob's first-born son? Most would say Reuben, but is that biblically true?

In Genesis, when Jacob fell in love it was with Rachel. However, being Laban's younger daughter, Laban tricked Jacob into marrying Leah. Sadly, after Rachel and Jacob marry, she is barren. However, years later, she has two sons, Joseph and Benjamin. So how do we know that Joseph is considered Jacob's first born? Firstly, because he was the first born of the woman that he loved and worked for years to marry. Secondly, there is no tribe of Joseph. Why? Because the first born is given a double portion of the inheritance. That is why the sons of Joseph, Ephram, and Manasseh, each are considered in the twelve tribes.

Some may argue that the tribe of Levi, being priests without a land inheritance caused the other two tribes to become necessary, but why were Joseph's sons chosen? Why were Rueben's sons not chosen? The first born was a very important position in the Jewish culture. Could this be the reason that Jesus was to be the first born?

Jesus also had to be born of God. He could not have been born of a man and have been the 'Son of God.' Having been born of Mary He could be called the Son of Man as well. Of course, the word 'man' in the New Testament often means mankind or humanity. In the God-Man, Jesus, we see a mixing of the divine nature of God the Father and the human nature of Mary. We find the perfect balance of the two natures. This is something only God can do, not humanity. This balance, this divine tension, is only in Jesus. Why is this important here? Because it is not just the balance of the two natures that is in question. Another question in the hypostatic union is found in Philippians 2:5-8: *Let this mind be in you, which was also in Christ Jesus: Who, being in the form of God, thought it not robbery to be equal with God: But made himself of no reputation, and took upon him the form of a servant, and was made in the likeness of men: And being found in fashion as a man, he humbled himself, and became obedient unto death, even the death of the cross.* So, the rub is not so much the two natures, though that is in the mix, but it is understanding what exactly Jesus did when He 'made Himself of no reputation.' The Greek word reputation is *kenoso* which can be translated *emptied oneself.* Here is the sticky part. What did Jesus empty Himself *of* when becoming incarnate? The historical, fundamental, theological position is the Jesus 'gave up the independent exercise of His divine attributes.' Here is one person's interpretation:

During the dispensation of the hypostatic union, our Lord Jesus Christ voluntarily restricted the independent use of His divine attributes in compliance with the Father's plan for the Incarnation and the First Advent. This means that Jesus Christ did not use the attributes of His divine nature to benefit Himself, to provide for Himself, to glorify Himself, or to act independently of the plan of God for the Church-age by any compromise of the spiritual life. One compromise of the human nature of Jesus Christ to the spiritual life, and there would not be any spiritual life in the Church Age.

The objectives of the dispensation of the hypostatic union were related to the human nature of Jesus Christ. To resist temptation, the human nature of Jesus Christ must not call on the divine nature for help. He had to use the four mechanics of the spiritual life to maintain His human perfection and to be qualified to go to the Cross and be judged for the sins of the world. During the dispensation of the hypostatic union, our Lord Jesus Christ voluntarily restricted the independent use of His divine attributes in compatibility with His own objectives and purpose in living among men with their limitations. By so doing, He established in His humanity a spiritual life which is the precedent for the Church Age. Christ voluntarily restricted the independent use of His divine attributes, but certain functions of deity continued to function, such as holding the universe together. Jesus Christ gave up the independent exercise of His divine attributes only during the dispensation of the hypostatic union. He did not give up His divine attributes – that is a heresy. (5)

My question for this answer is: When do the members of the Godhead act independently of one another? Does this not go directly against the idea of oneness in the Godhead? If anything is truly one, it is the Godhead. They are one in mind, one in thought, one in purpose, one in action, one in everything. Therefore, there is no independent exercise of anything in the Godhead. So, what did Jesus give up? I believe that there is merit to the fundamental position, but I believe that it is more than what is written in the position. Jesus gave up 'being' God when he became a man. He was still the God-Man, but he did not have the divine attributes at His independent disposal which, He never had anyway. The Trinity always worked completely together. Jesus truly became incarnate, God in the flesh, with only God the Father, His Father, to make Him different from us. Therefore, He was born sinless like Adam, yet, he did not have the power that resides in God alone when he was a man. This includes the 'veiling' of His Glory. Part of the reason I say this is the context of Philippians 2:5-8 which says:

Have this mind among yourselves, which is yours in

Christ Jesus, who, though he was in the form of God, did not count equality with God a thing to be grasped, but emptied himself, taking the form of a servant, being born in the likeness of men. And being found in human form he humbled himself and became obedient unto death, even death on a cross. (RSV).

There are many versions to look at when translating the Scripture, the RSV here lays out that Jesus did not think that being equal with God was a thing to be 'grasped' or held on to at all costs. We are then told that Jesus emptied Himself. In context, therefore, Jesus emptied Himself of equality with God. He did this so He could become a man. What does that mean for Jesus? The mystery is that He gave up 'being God' so that He could become human. I am not sure that the Scriptures lay out clearly what that all entailed.

Some will say that this is heresy because of the historical, fundamental, ingrained theology that we study. Biblically, I believe that this is the only thing that really makes sense. There are too many Scriptures that indicate that Jesus was a man when He was here. Luke 4:1 *says that Jesus was full of the Holy Spirit and was led by the Spirit into the wilderness.* Why did God need to be filled with God? And then why was God led by God? Hebrews 5:7-10, says: During the days of Jesus' life on earth, he offered up prayers and petitions with fervent cries and tears to the one who could save him from death, and he was heard because of his reverent submission. Son though he was, he learned obedience from what he suffered and, once made perfect, he became the source of eternal salvation for all who obey him and was designated by God to be high priest in the order of Melchizedek. Luke 2:52 says: *And Jesus kept increasing in wisdom and stature, and in favor with God and men.* This is an interesting Scripture. How was Jesus *made perfect* or complete? He was tempted in all points, like us, yet he did not sin. (Hebrews 4:15) This was necessary so that Jesus could do what Adam did not do, and, therefore, take back what Adam lost when he sinned. Why was Adam's sin different than Eve's? Adam knew without deception, and he chose to sin. Jesus knew without deception and chose NOT to sin. Romans 4-6 describes this fully, as well as the passage in 1 Corinthians 15. All these verses demonstrate the reason why Jesus must become a man. Only in His manhood could he do what Adam should have done in the garden. Look at these words from Hebrews 5, *once made perfect....* The correct choice by Jesus to obey God in His humanity changed everything for us. Now His obedience opens the door of salvation for us. His obedience and triumph over the evil one defeated the authority of Satan, and then Jesus gave that to us. *'Behold, I have given you authority to tread on serpents and scorpions, and over all the power of the enemy, and nothing will injure you.'* Luke 10:19. We can now do what God intended Adam to do in the garden. We can obey God and chose His will over our own. We can choose good over evil by listening to the Holy Spirit and choosing what He tells us is the will of God.

Back to Hebrews 4:15, it is interesting that God learned and increased in wisdom. This is where I believe that the historical position gets it right. He did give up His divine attributes as a man, but He could not give up something that He never had, which is the independent exercise of those attributes. I believe that the historical position is concerned about taking away from Jesus's Godhood. However, Philippians answers that when it says that He made Himself of no reputation. Jesus willingly, humbly 'emptied Himself' so that He could be fully man and experience everything that we experience. This did not diminish His Godhood. This is what I see in the Scripture describing Jesus: He was the only human who was 100% submitted to the Holy Spirit, 100% of the time. We experience moments of 100% submission, when all our being is submitted to the Holy Spirit, and in those moments, we are like Jesus. For us, this seems difficult, to be 100% submitted, 100% of the time, however, it is not impossible. This is a partial testimony from Charles Finney, about submission to the Holy Spirit and His power. *"Sometimes I would find myself, in a great measure, empty of this power. I would go out and visit and find that I made no saving impression. I would exhort and pray, with the same result. I would then set apart a day for private fasting and prayer, fearing that this power had departed from me, and would inquire anxiously after the reason of this apparent emptiness. After humbling myself, and crying out for help, the power would return upon me with all its freshness. This has been the experience of my life.*(4). So, when Finney felt the power of the Holy Spirit begin to wane he fasted and prayed until it returned. Please read the historical facts and testimony of Finney. This man 'walked in the Spirit.'

There have been those in some parts of Christianity who have taken the Kenosis too far saying that we can be like 'God.' This is where they stray into heresy and the temptation of the evil one who tempted Eve with the same idea. Let me say clearly here, there are ways that humans are like God, but Jehovah God is NOT like us. He is altogether different. We are made in His image and likeness, but He is NOT like us, we are like Him. We will NEVER be Him. Because Jesus was different in that He was the God man, some things about Him were different than us. I believe that this is true for Jesus laying down His life. Jesus, as the God-Man had the ability to hold onto life until all that needed to be accomplished on the Cross was completed. Jesus said in John 10, *"I am the good shepherd, and know my sheep, and am known of mine. As the Father knows me, even so know I the Father: and I lay down my life for the sheep. And other sheep I have, which are not of this fold: them also I must bring, and they shall hear my voice; and there shall be one-fold, and one shepherd. Therefore, my Fathers love me, because I lay down my life, that I might take it again. No man takes it from me, but I lay it down of myself. I have power to lay it down, and I have power to take it again. This commandment have I received of my Father."*

Compare John to Isaiah 52:13-15, *Behold, my servant shall prosper, he shall be exalted and lifted up, and shall be very high. As many were astonished at him—his appearance was so marred, beyond human semblance, and his form beyond that of the sons of men—so shall he startle many nations; kings shall shut their mouths because of him for that which has not been told them they shall see, and that which they have not heard they shall understand.*

What's the point? Jesus was beaten so badly that He should have died. You and I would have died. Hebrews 12:3-4, provides another clue to this context: *'Consider him who endured from sinners such hostility against himself, so that you may not grow weary or fainthearted. In your struggle against sin you have not yet resisted to the point of shedding your blood.'* How can the writer say this when many believers had shed their blood? Stephen was stoned, which I am sure caused some bloodshed. The context may be that none of the believers he was writing to had shed their blood, but I believe in the context of talking about Jesus, the writer of Hebrews compares what we suffered and what Jesus suffered. Jesus suffered greatly and beyond what we could have endured, until all was completed. This is why He said on the cross, 'It is finished,' and THEN He 'gave up the ghost.' Jesus suffered through what would have killed us because He did have control over His death as a command from the Father. This is because He was the God-Man.

Another concern of the modern theological thinking is whether Jesus was a man. We mostly talk about the deity of Jesus and rarely talk about His humanity. In the first century, the opposite was true. Everyone knew that Jesus was a man. They thought He was a prophet, a miracle worker, but still a man. Some were even offended by Him like when He went to Nazareth in Mark 6, and Luke 4.

Mark 6:1-6 Jesus, *went out from there and came into His hometown; and His disciples followed Him. When the Sabbath came, He began to teach in the synagogue; and the many listeners were astonished, saying, "Where did this man get these things, and what is this wisdom given to Him, and such miracles as these performed by His hands? Is not this the carpenter, the son of Mary, and brother of James and Joses and Judas and Simon? Are not His sisters here with us?" And they took offense at Him. Jesus said to them, "A prophet is not without honor except in his hometown and among his own relatives and in his own household." And He could do no miracle there except that He laid His hands on a few sick people and healed them. And He wondered at their unbelief.*

Luke 4:16-31, *He then went to Naz'a·reth, where he had been brought up, and according to his custom on the Sabbath day, he entered the synagogue and stood up to read. So, the scroll of the prophet Isaiah was handed to him, and he opened the scroll and found the place where it was written: "Jehovah's spirit is upon me, because he anointed me to declare good news to the poor. He sent me*

53

to proclaim liberty to the captives and a recovery of sight to the blind, to send the crushed ones away free, to preach Jehovah's acceptable year." With that he rolled up the scroll, handed it back to the attendant, and sat down; and the eyes of all in the synagogue were intently fixed on him. Then he began to say to them: "Today this Scripture that you just heard* is fulfilled. "And they all began to give favorable witness about him and to be amazed at the gracious words coming out of his mouth, and they were saying: "This is a son of Joseph, is it not? At this he said to them: "No doubt you will apply this saying to me, 'Physician, cure yourself. Do also here in your home territory the things we have heard were done in Ca·per'na·um.'" So, he said: "Truly I tell you that no prophet is accepted in his home territory. For instance, I tell you in truth: There were many widows in Israel in the days of E·li'jah when heaven was shut up for three years and six months, and a great famine came on all the land. Yet E·li'jah was sent to none of those women, but only to a widow in Zar'e·phath in the land of Si'don. Also, there were many lepers in Israel in the time of E·li'sha the prophet; yet not one of them was cleansed, only Na'a·man the Syrian." Now all those hearing these things in the synagogue became filled with anger, and they rose up and rushed him outside the city, and they led him to the brow of the mountain* on which their city had been built, in order to throw him down headlong. But he went right through their midst and continued on his way.

Putting these two passages together gives us more complete picture of what happened in Nazareth with Jesus that day. They were offended because they knew Him and did not believe that the kid that grew up with them in Nazareth was who He appeared to be. Would this event have gone differently if there was any doubt in their minds that Jesus was the Son of God? To them He was just a grown-up kid that they knew, and therefore, could not be who everyone else was saying He was.

When Jesus was teaching in John 10, the Jews were questioning Him. In verses 27-33, we read: *My sheep listen to my voice; I know them, and they follow me. I give them eternal life, and they shall never perish; no one will snatch them out of my hand. My Father, who has given them to me, is greater than all[c]; no one can snatch them out of my Father's hand. I and the Father are one. "Again his Jewish opponents picked up stones to stone him, but Jesus said to them, "I have shown you many good works from the Father. For which of these do you stone me?" "We are not stoning you for any good work," they replied, "but for blasphemy, because you, a mere man, claim to be God."*

Here we see that the Jews totally understood what He was saying. They knew He was equating Himself with God. They, however, were convinced that He was just a man. So, these verses and others (which you can look up) demonstrate that in the first century the issue of Jesus's Godhood was at question, not His manhood. Today, we struggle with His humanity, and therefore, focus more on His Godhood. This is a detraction from who Jesus was. While here on earth, He was a man. Peter says that He is our example to follow in suffering, but also in so many other things. I have hope for a better walk with God, under the power of the Holy Spirit, because of the example of Jesus.

What is the conclusion for this matter? There is a divine balance, not only in the Hypostatic Union, but in who Jesus was while He was on earth. These two pieces are tied together. It brings hope, and even balance to me, when I realize that Jesus walked as we walk, ate as we eat, prayed as we pray, suffered as we suffer and was tempted as we are tempted. Submitting to the Father in the Holy Spirit and using the sword of the Scriptures was the way that Jesus overcame and persevered while He was here. He literally was a walking balance of divinity and humanity. Though we cannot be as Jesus was, we, too, can have the balance of divinity (the Holy Spirit) and humanity, (our human nature) like He did. We, too, can 'walk in the Spirit' and have the 'mind of Christ.'

Michael Card, who has a Master's degree in biblical studies, wrote a song called "The Mystery" that has lyrics describing the Kenosis. I think that his assessment is spot on in the words at the end of each stanza. Please take the time now to look up the lyrics to this song and read Michael Card's amazing words.

So then what is the balance for us as believers today? Is there a balance that we can find in the human and the divine, here, and now, in this life we live in this physical realm? I believe that there is, and that balance will be given more context in a following chapter called submission. We all are human, and those of us who believe are now partly divine by the presence of the Holy Spirit within us. Those of us who believe are now born again, not of our will, but of God's will and by His Spirit. We are now adopted, and we have become the children of God. We are humans, and we are co-heirs with Jesus the first born. We now have direct access by the blood of Jesus to the very throne of our Heavenly Father. Romans 5:1-11 and Hebrews 4:14-16. How can we balance all that we have been given by God as our divine inheritance and our struggle with our humanity? We can see what we need to do and how we need to accomplish it by a better understanding of Jesus as presented to us in the Old Testament prophecies and the Gospels. Jesus walked the tightrope of humanity and divinity, even in difficult moments, without falling off the rope and into the chasm. I know that much of what I have learned that is shared in this book is because of a quest I went on years ago to be more like Jesus in every way. One of the great truths that I knew but rediscovered in a new and positive way was that God's goal, while we are here, is to bring us into the image of His Son, Jesus. 2 Corinthians 3:18, Romans 8:29, Colossians 3:10, 1 Corinthians 15:49, Ephesians 4:24. I will not go into any detail about what this quest meant for me and how I was changed because of the quest. What I want to do here is encourage you, the reader, to take up this quest for yourself. I want to encourage you to discover that God is more than we can think or imagine, and that there is no one like Jesus for us in all the earth.

COULD JESUS HAVE SINNED?

This is a theological nightmare! As God, the answer would be a resounding NO! But as man, things get a little tricky. The Scriptures teach that Jesus was tempted like we are but did not sin. This theological question also moves over into the area of philosophy because there are so many twists and turns as we think about the concept of whether Jesus could have sinned. Here's a question: Are the temptations real if you are not tempted? Since most theologians believe that God cannot sin, because it is not in His nature to sin, then, also follows that God would be impervious to temptation. So, can God be tempted? The clear answer is no. But God also cannot suffer, or feel pain, or hunger, or longing, (at least not the way that we do). But Jesus felt all these things as a man. Before Jesus came this was a heartfelt cry of humanity when suffering occurred. This is long passage, but listen to the cry of Job,

"If it is a matter of power, behold, He is the strong one! And if it is a matter of justice, who can summon Him? "Though I am righteous, my mouth will condemn me; Though I am guiltless, He will declare me guilty. "I am guiltless; I do not take notice of myself; I despise my life. "It is all one; therefore, I say, 'He destroys the guiltless and the wicked.' "If the scourge kills suddenly, He mocks

*the despair of the innocent. "The earth is given into the hand of the wicked He covers the faces of its judges. If it is not He, then who is it? "Now my days are swifter than a runner; They flee away, they see no good. "They slip by like reed boats, like an eagle that swoops on its prey. "Though I say, 'I will forget my complaint, I will leave off my sad countenance and be cheerful,' I am afraid of all my pains I know that You will not acquit me. "I am accounted wicked, why then should I toil in vain? "If I should wash myself with snow And cleanse my hands with lye, Yet You would plunge me into the pit, And my own clothes would abhor me. "For He is not a man as I am that I may answer Him, That we may go to court together. **There is no mediator between us, Who may lay his hand upon us both**. "Let Him remove His rod from me, And let not dread of Him terrify me. Then I would speak and not fear Him;* (Job 9:19-35).

This has changed now with the advent of Jesus. *For there is one God, and one mediator also between God and men, the man Christ Jesus, who gave Himself as a ransom for all, the testimony given at the proper time.* (2 Timothy 2:5-6). Now Jesus has become a man and *has* experienced all these things so He can understand. So, as God, Jesus could not sin, but as man it reasons out that it had to be possible for there to even be a temptation. What would be the point of Satan tempting Jesus if there was no possibility that He could sin? Why does Hebrews 4 say that Jesus was perfected by His struggles? Jesus being able to resist temptation and remain sinless is the reason why He is called the second Adam. Jesus walked the perfect balance of temptation and perseverance, of humanity and Deity. Imagine the tension that He kept in balance which is most likely the reason there is so much mystery in this question.

CHAPTER FOUR

Liberty and Law:
The Balance of the New
and the Old Covenant

The question of liberty and law is widely debated. Some people call this conflict the grace verses law issue. As we dive into this delicate balance, I will try to give some background and some nuances to this. The main struggles with this issue will be discussed a little further in the chapter. Between liberty and law, which one holds sway over the Era of Grace that we are currently experiencing? Some say that we must follow the law, and so there are believers who observe the feasts and times of the Old Testament. Some of these believers in the Gospel of Jesus are Messianic Jews. These folks have a depth of understanding of the Old Testament and the culture of Israel. For them, it is not a question of following some of the things that we consider to be 'the Law.' These things are part of their culture. Some of them do not do them out of obligation, but out of love for the Savior who was also Jewish. There is a significant difference in doing something out of obligation and doing the same thing out of love. Isaiah. 1: 11-14:

"What are your multiplied sacrifices to Me?" Says the Lord. "I have had enough of burnt offerings of rams And the fat of fed cattle; And I take no pleasure in the blood of bulls, lambs or goats. "When you come to appear before Me, Who requires of you this trampling of My courts? "Bring your worthless offerings no longer, incense is an abomination to Me. New moon and sabbath, the calling of assemblies—I cannot endure iniquity and the solemn assembly. "I hate your new moon festivals and your appointed feasts, They have become a burden to Me; I am weary of bearing them."

Israel had fallen out of love with the Lord and into vain offerings of obligation. Lest we judge Israel too harshly let's see what the church did in the first century. Revelation 2:4-5:

But I have this against you, that you have left your first love. Therefore, remember from where you have fallen, and repent and do the deeds you did at first; or else I am coming to you and will remove your lamp stand out of its place—unless you repent.

Settling into a situation where things are done out of obligation is religion not relationship. Wives are very good at helping husbands with this in the marriage relationship. Even after marriage they desire to be romanced. Now, in the New Covenant, the Holy Spirit helps us with this in our relationship with the Father. One of my friends said that the Holy Spirit is much like our wives in marriage, easily offended and always right. In spite of the 'Helper' having come, we can still resist and fall into obligation.

One of the best arguments that Scripture gives for keeping the law is Matthew 5:17-19:

"Do not think that I came to abolish the Law or the Prophets; I did not come to abolish but to fulfill. For truly I say to you, until heaven and earth pass away, not the smallest letter or stroke shall pass from the Law until all is accomplished. Whoever then annuls one of the least of these commandments, and teaches others to do the same, shall be called least in the kingdom of heaven; but whoever keeps and teaches them, he shall be called great in the kingdom of heaven.

Jesus then goes on to quote some of the Ten Commandments. No one would say today, in the church, in the Age of Grace, that it is okay worship other 'gods,' make and worship an idol, blaspheme the Name of Jehovah, dismiss the day of rest, dishonor parents, murder, lie, steal, covet, or commit adultery. So what laws are we saying that we should not keep? Jesus has done what He said that He was going to do. He came and fulfilled all the law's requirements and the prophecies concerning the Messiah. Jesus became the 'Lamb slain before the foundation of the world' so we do not have to do the blood sacrifices any longer. Therefore, the ceremonial laws that were to be performed as a foreshadow of the coming Messiah no longer are necessary to continue in the New Covenant. Having said that there are many moral laws that are incapsulated in the two greatest commands that have never been done away. In fact, Jesus takes the moral laws in the Sermon on the Mount and expands them to be more than just outward obedience. He teaches that the breaking of these laws starts with what is happening inside us as humans. That is why Jesus taught:

"It is not what enters into the mouth that defiles the man, but what proceeds out of the mouth, this defiles the man."Then the disciples came and said to Him, "Do You know that the Pharisees were offended when they heard this statement?" But He answered and said, "Every plant which My heavenly Father did not plant shall be uprooted. Let them alone; they are blind guides of the blind. And if a blind man guides a blind man, both will fall into a pit." Peter said to Him, "Explain the parable to us." Jesus said, "Are you still lacking in understanding also? Do you not understand that everything that goes into the mouth passes into the stomach, and is eliminated? But the things that proceed out of the mouth come from the heart, and those defile the man. For out of the heart come evil thoughts, murders, adulteries, fornications, thefts, false witness, slanders. These are the things which defile the man; but to eat with unwashed hands does not defile the man." Matthew 15:11-20.

Because their devotion became religious, the Jewish people were obsessed with the letter of the law rather than the spirit of the law. The letter of the law examines the law looking for loopholes to do whatever it is that you want, but the spirit of the law, driven by love, understands relationship and, therefore, follows the two greatest commands easily. The letter of the law and keeping it, induces pride and a critical, judgmental spirit toward those who do not keep the letter of the law. This is why Jesus said, *"For I say to you that unless your righteousness surpasses that of the scribes and Pharisees, you will not enter the kingdom of heaven."* Matthew 5:20.

When we look at the New Testament and the book of Acts specifically, we see the issue of law and grace in the earliest beginnings of the church. When we read the book of Acts, we read it as a narrative, but we often do not realize the number of years that transpire in the book. When we read the book of Galatians, chapters one and two, and compare it to the book of Acts we discover that there are several years that have gone by. Acts 9:19-26 occurs over a three-year period according to Galatians 1:13-18, but when we read the text it seems like it all happens in a week. Galatians then tells us that there are fourteen years between Acts 9:26 and Acts 15:1. It is important to understand this because we see that some time passed, but not too much time before this issue became one that most theologians believe resulted in the first church council. In Acts 15, the church at Jerusalem held a council to talk about the issue of grace and law. This controversy was mainly centered on whether to circumcise those Gentiles who were coming to Christ. It did take some time to develop as demonstrated by the number of years that passed. Settling doctrinal issues started here but continued through the centuries. There were many synods that were established to settle doctrinal issues that had risen in the church. Often there is disdain for doctrine and theology by some, I believe mostly because there is a lack of understanding why these doctrines developed and how important they are to understand. Many doctrines developed out of these church councils where there was a refutation of the heresies that were developing in the church. The grace, law doctrinal issue was the first one that the church had to correct because some of the people from Judea were preaching that a person had to be circumcised to be saved. Why that was the issue for these people is hard to say. Maybe because circumcision was a sign of the old covenant, and they wanted it to be a sign of the new covenant as well. Over the years this controversy grew into a works mentally where a person had to work to earn their salvation. Though the first century was about circumcision, the actual controversy remains the same. In Galatians 1 and 2, Paul speaks directly to this issue. In fact, it is one of the things that comes out in almost all of the epistles of Paul. Look at Galatians 2:15-16:

*"We who are Jews by birth and not sinful Gentiles know that a person is not justified by the works of the law, but by faith in Jesus Christ. So we, too, have put our faith in Christ Jesus that we may be justified by faith in Christ and not by the works of the law, **because by the works of the law no one will be justified.**"*

If we read this verse and understand what it says, then my question is why is there any controversy? The part of the verse that is bold seems really clear to me. This is not the only verse or passage where Paul talks about justification by faith. Keeping the law without faith is okay, and your life will be blessed, but *'without faith it is impossible to please God.'* Hebrews 11

Years ago, when I was in college and a young believer, as in not mature or experienced, I worked with a man who was not a believer in the Gospel of Jesus. I tried to witness to him, and he was always cordial but resistant to the Gospel. I was surprised because I realized as a young man the importance of faith in Jesus to cleanse me from my sin. After getting to know the man and learning about him and his family, I realized that he had a morality that was uncommon even all those years ago. He, his wife, and their children lived by the tenants of biblical faith without receiving Jesus as their Savior. This was revealed to me in one of his statements. He basically said, "Why do I need Jesus when I live my life the way I do, and my life is blessed?" I did not have an answer for him in that moment. Like I said, I was young and inexperienced at eighteen years old. This story is an illustration of Paul's proclamation in Galatians 2:16. Your life may be blessed, but you are not justified by the works that you do. You can only be justified by believing in Jesus and what He did for all of us. My friend's life was blessed for following the commands, but in the end we all have to stand before God and give an account about what John 3:17-18 says: '*17 For God did not send the Son into the world to judge the world, but that the world might be saved through Him. 18 He who believes in Him is not judged; he who does not believe has been judged already, because he has not believed in the name of the only begotten Son of God.*'

Part of the controversy arises from the Bible itself. The book of James was one of the last books to be canonized by the church. The church council that recognized James as canonical was the Synod of Laodicea in 363AD, though it was first recognized by Eusebius, earlier in the 4th century. Part of the reason for the late recognition was the question of authorship of the book. Though now believed to have been written by the half-brother of Jesus, it was often thought to be pseudonymous. Whatever you think, there is little doubt that the text seems to advocate for a salvation by works and keeping the law. Here is the passage from James 2 in the KJV:

14 What doth it profit, my brethren, though a man say he hath faith, and have not works? can faith save him? 15 If a brother or sister be naked, and destitute of daily food, 16 And one of you say unto them, Depart in peace, be ye warmed and filled; notwithstanding ye give them not those things which are needful to the body; what doth it profit? 17 Even so faith, if it hath not works, is dead, being alone. 18 Yea, a man may say, Thou hast faith, and I have works: shew me thy faith without thy works, and I will shew thee my faith by my works. 19 Thou believest that there is one

God; thou doest well: the devils also believe, and tremble. 20 But wilt thou know, O vain man, that faith without works is dead? 21 Was not Abraham our father justified by works, when he had offered Isaac his son upon the altar? 22 Seest thou how faith wrought with his works, and by works was faith made perfect? 23 And the scripture was fulfilled which saith, Abraham believed God, and it was imputed unto him for righteousness: and he was called the Friend of God. 24 Ye see then how that by works a man is justified, and not by faith only. 25 Likewise also was not Rahab the harlot justified by works, when she had received the messengers, and had sent them out another way? 26 For as the body without the spirit is dead, so faith without works is dead also.

Verse 14 in the NASB 1995 reads, 14 *'What use is it, my brethren, if someone says he has faith, but he has no works? Can that faith save him?'* There is a foot note by the word 'that' which says the Greek should literally read, 'What use is it, my brethren, if someone says he has faith, but he has no works? Can *the* faith save him?' I find it interesting that major doctrines of Scripture can hinge on one word from the text which, in this case, is an article. However, the article does define the word faith for those who believe that faith is the basis for salvation. Here is a point that needs to be understood when looking at the whole of Scripture. We need to keep in mind what Peter said about the prophetic words of the Old Testament which applies to all Scripture. 2 Peter 1:19-21:

19 So we have the prophetic word made more sure, to which you do well to pay attention as to a lamp shining in a dark place, until the day dawns and the morning star arises in your hearts. 20 But know this first of all, that no prophecy of Scripture is a matter of one's own interpretation, 21 for no prophecy was ever made by an act of human will, but men moved by the Holy Spirit spoke from God.

No prophecy of Scripture is of any private or personal interpretation or cannot be interpreted alone (privately) without considering the rest of Scripture. And we can add that this applies to all of Scripture as well. What does this mean since there are literally thousands of interpretations of prophecy and Scripture. What I believe is that we should look at all of Scripture not just build a doctrine from one or two verses. When we look at what James says in James 2, and compare the multitude of other verses about salvation being by grace through faith, or belief, what we find is that the passage in James makes the most sense when we see verse 14 in the NASB version. The important thing to remember about the KJV and the NASB is that they are what is called a 'word by word translation.' These versions are not the only word for word translations available. However, a lot of the other translations, and especially newer versions, are what is called a meaning for meaning, thought for thought, or paraphrase because there are words added to make the English 'flow.' That is why the KJV, and a lot of the NASB, sound like Yoda from Star Wars. Paraphrases can be rich in some ways, but there is a statement about language translations that applies called, 'lost in translation.' This basically means that no language perfectly translates to another. This is the reason why the KJV and NASB specifically are a word for word translation. The object is to hold to what the original Hebrew, Aramaic, and Greek words mean in English.

Back to James 2. James is talking about a faith that is in words only. As an example, some people say that they are Christians when it is convenient for them. If you look at their life, without condemning, you see no fruit that is a consequence of a true salvation experience. What you do see are a lot of words in specific moments about being a Christian. What you do not see is consistent action taken as a demonstration of faith. This is what James is addressing in chapter two. He is calling into question whether some people who talk a lot about faith are really 'in faith.' Jesus told us in Matthew 7:15-20, *'by their fruit you will know them.'* James was not advocating works and law over grace and faith salvation. He was saying that there are pretenders, and this is a way to discern true faith from words faith.

LIBERTY

Liberty given to believers in the New Testament/ Covenant is not a license to sin. Romans 6:1: *What shall we say then? Are we to continue in sin so that grace may increase? 2 May it never be! How shall we who died to sin still live in it? 6 knowing this, that our old self was crucified with Him, in order that our body of sin might be done away with, so that we would no longer be slaves to sin; 7 for he who has died is freed from sin. 12 Therefore do not let sin reign in your mortal body so that you obey its lusts, 13 and do not go on presenting the members of your body to sin as instruments of unrighteousness; but present yourselves to God as those alive from the dead, and your members as instruments of righteousness to God. 14 For sin shall not be master over you, for you are not under law but under grace. 15 What then? Shall we sin because we are not under law but under grace? May it never be! 16 Do you not know that when you present yourselves to someone as slaves for obedience, you are slaves of the one whom you obey, either of sin resulting in death, or of obedience resulting in righteousness?*

The liberty of the New Testament/Covenant is *a liberty from the guilt and penalty of sin*. We no longer must live in fear or doubt about whether we have done our 'duty,' kept all the commands to the letter, or sinned too much for God to forgive us. Love casts out fear. John 4:15: *Whoever confesses that Jesus is the Son of God, God abides in him, and he in God. 16 We have come to know and have believed the love which God has for us. God is love, and the one who abides in love abides in God, and God abides in him. 17 By this, love is perfected with us, so that we may have confidence in the day of judgment; because as He is, so also are we in this world. 18 There is no fear in love; but perfect love casts out fear, because fear involves punishment, and the one who fears is not perfected in love.*

Now, as believers, we serve God out of love. John 4:19: *We love, because He first loved us. Love, respect, honesty, and Godly fear are four motivators for a life of righteousness.* We also mature to understand that what God has designed for us in creating us as humans is what is best for us. When we understand that God is motivated by His great love for us, we come to realize what John was talking about in 1 John 5:2*: By this we know that we love the children of God, when we love God and observe His commandments. For this is the love of God, that we keep His commandments;* **and His commandments are not burdensome.** The KJV says that the commandments are not grievous. We are not grieved in our spirits about the commands because we have learned that they are what is best for us. They are not roadblocks to keep us out, they are guardrails to keep us from going over the edge and into some form of pain. In this place there is no conflict between liberty and law, or grace and works. They function together as they were meant to before the fall in Genesis 3. This is the divine tension and balance between liberty and law.

CHAPTER FIVE

Submission:
The Balance Between
Leading and Following

Does everybody want to be a leader? The answer seems obvious - NO. Does everyone want to be follower? Definitely not. So, do leaders always lead, every time? No ... good leaders have to also be good followers. Think of the military chain of command. If I am a captain then I am a leader, or at least in the position of leadership. I may even be a really good leader, but when the major gives me a command, I have to become a follower. This is where I believe that the divine tension holds this relationship between leading and following in balance. I must trust my leader enough to be a good follower. If I disobey my major, then I am said to be in a place of insubordination, and I may end up in the brig. Also, if I cannot follow the commands of my leader, should my followers be expected to follow me? Would I question their sanity if they were insubordinate? In *humanity*, there actually must be a "chain of command" for things to get done. If I am a captain, and I have three lieutenants under my command with twenty sergeants of various ranks, and two hundred privates, does that make me better or superior, as a human, than those under my command? Of course not. No human is better or superior to any other human.

All humans are created equal before God. If we could strip way the flesh and stand with each other in the spirit, I believe that our equality would become obvious. In the flesh, are there specific things that certain people can achieve better than others? Of course! We give away gold metals to people of superior strength or skill every two years at the Winter or Summer Olympic Games. Am I physically stronger than my wife who is 5'3", and I am 6'5" and grew up on a farm? Obviously, does that make me superior to her in the ways that matter before God? No, it does not. There are ways that my wife is superior to me. She is an excellent planner, and I fly by the seat of my pants, so who do you think plans vacations? Is everything we need packed and accounted for before we go on a trip? Only if my wife is doing the planning. She is definitely superior to me in planning. In our standing before God is she, therefore, superior? I don't think so. In whether Jesus died for us is she superior? Not at all. To me, in all the ways that matter to God, once we get to Heaven, we are equal. Again, once the flesh is stripped away, it is revealed that we are equal.

I seriously doubt that God is only going to judge the leaders. They may get a more difficult judgement based on the way they have led. They may even be judged more harshly for not leading well. (Matthew 23:14, James 3:1) The followers also must stand before God and give an account. I believe that if I submit out of respect for the leader above me, though I disagree and respectfully disagree in conversation with my leader, then as long as I am not breaking a command of God, I am free from the judgement of my actions commanded by my leader. Would God give a command to destroy a city with fire and then judge us for burning it at His command? On the flip side, some followers think that they are leaders, but they are just rebellious and stubborn. I have had conversations with usurpers, and they criticize leaders but put forth no plan to lead. When you ask how they would do the leading you get, I don't know, just not this way. These people will face the Lord to answer for their rebellion.

Having said all that, this chapter is about leading and following. So, what are the qualities of a good leader? Can anyone be a leader? Is there an order in humanity, in the church, that God has laid out for us to follow? What is the biblical understanding of submission? What I want to do is lay out what the Bible teaches, and the conclusion will demonstrate why there is a divine tension and balance in this topic.

The qualities of a good leader.

A good leader is a person who understands authority. One of the most interesting leaders described in the Scriptures is found in Matthew 8:5-13:

And when Jesus entered Capernaum, a centurion came to Him, imploring Him, and saying, "Lord, my servant is lying paralyzed at home, fearfully tormented." Jesus said to him, "I will come and heal him." But the centurion said, "Lord, I am not worthy for You to come under my roof, but just say the word, and my servant will be healed. For I also am a man under authority, with soldiers under me; and I say to this one, 'Go!' and he goes, and to another, 'Come!' and he comes, and to my slave, 'Do this!' and he does it." Now when Jesus heard this, He marveled and said to those who were following, "Truly I say to you, I have not found such great faith with anyone in Israel. I say to you that many will come from east and west, and recline at the table with Abraham, Isaac, and Jacob in the kingdom of heaven; but the sons of the kingdom will be cast out into the outer darkness; in that place there will be weeping and gnashing of teeth." And Jesus said to the centurion, "Go; it shall be done for you as you have believed." And the servant was healed that very moment.

There are a lot of differing opinions about what a centurion was in the 1st century Roman army. Some say the word implies one hundred, but another source says that the word was because a centurion led centuries which we today call sentries. The Greek word is, *hekatontarchēs,* and it is a conjunction of two words meaning one hundred and leader. Some sources say that they led between sixty to one hundred soldiers. Whatever the number, the man was an officer in the Roman army. What this un-named Roman officer says to Jesus is astounding. Firstly, he comes to Jesus and implores that Jesus heal his servant. The first thing that you see in the text is that this Roman officer calls Jesus, "Lord." The word Lord is a title in this context and is the Greek word *kyrios.* One of the meanings is: *a title of honor, an expressive of respect and reverence.* The person using this title is a Roman centurion, a man whose responsibility is to insure the Roman rule in the province of Judea. Jesus was a nobody Jewish man from a small town and an insignificant family. Why is the Centurion using the word Lord important here? He recognized authority. He was a man in position of authority, a leader, and he recognized the authority that Jesus carried. When a person has God-given authority, it can be recognized by someone who is discerning.

In the story, the Centurion recognizes authority, and he recognizes the power that it carries. That is why Jesus is amazed when the centurion says, 'Just speak the word.' He recognized, respected, and believed in the authority of Jesus. Why does this story have merit in this context of divine balance and mystery? The centurion held the balance in his own life. He understood leading and following. He understood authority and submission. The way I see it biblically, you forfeit the 'right' to lead if you cannot submit. Tell me how a person who refuses to submit recognizes the Lordship of Jesus? And I am not talking about submission in the marriage relationship. Even Jesus submitted to the leading of the Holy Spirit and His Father.

The Godhead submits to each other because humility has no problem with submission.

Good leaders are humble and understand submission. Good leaders have empathy and love for those that they lead. I believe that God wants us to lead with love and walk in truth. That was the title to a message I preached from Corinthians a few years ago. 'Lead with Love, Walk in Truth.' These two concepts are not mutually exclusive of one another. We can, as Paul reminds us, 'speak the truth in love.' Ephesians 4:13-16:

'until we all attain to the unity of the faith, and of the knowledge of the Son of God, to a mature man (human), to the measure of the stature which belongs to the fullness of Christ. As a result, we are no longer to be children, tossed here and there by waves and carried about by every wind of doctrine, by the trickery of people, by craftiness in deceitful scheming; **but speaking the truth in love,** *we are to grow up in all aspects into Him who is the head, that is, Christ, from whom the whole body, being fitted and held together by what every joint supplies, according to the proper working of each individual part,* **causes the growth of the body for the building up of itself in love.**

Good leaders know the truth and are not afraid to walk in the truth. However, when they speak the truth to others, they should speak the truth in love. This story gives us another quality about good leaders. Good leaders care about those who follow. The centurion came to Jesus for healing, not for himself, or a member of his family, but for his servant. What was the motivating factor for this Roman officer to humble himself and ask for healing for his servant? Love. He had a deep regard for those who were under his leadership.

Years ago, I worked in management for UPS. Needless to say, I was a leader by position, so my employees 'had' to listen to me. I wanted them to want to listen, not have to listen. Now my faith was in the mix so one of my characteristics was not to lie. I had one of my employees tell me I was hobbled as a management person because I would not lie to them about anything. Since 'every supervisor lied' he felt it gave him the upper hand in our relationship. I felt my not lying engendered trust. In fact, this same employee had learned to trust me so much that he turned his production level around by three hours less per day. One of my goals as a supervisor was to develop relationships with my employees and then demonstrate that I cared by taking care of them whenever I could. Sometimes that was just listening, and other times it meant that I had to go out and work with them side by side. If I had a driver that needed to be done early, I would ride with him, and we would do one person's work with two people, that way I could assure that he was done early. Over the months, this relationship worked, and it built trust and respect amongst my employees. When other management people would ask me about what I did and why, I would tell them that I wanted to have all my employees 'in my back pocket' so that they worked as hard when I was not around as they did when I was around because they knew I cared and had their best interest at heart. When the chips were down, which was often at UPS, my employees dug in and got the job done well. Was I a leader by position? I was. But I treated my people as equals and almost like volunteers, so I did not have to exercise my positional authority for them to work hard for me. Because I had a high regard for my people, they came to have a high regard for me. Once, when my manager was covering another shift, he needed extra people to come into work early. Early meant 3:00 a.m. He called me after my evening shift was over and wanted me to call 'my' people and get three to come into work at 3:00 a.m. I asked him why he had not called already. He was the manager and had more authority than me in the building. He told me he had called seven and no one said "yes" to come in at 3:00 a.m. so he wanted me to call and 'work my magic.' I laughed and said, "Let me call." I knew what he meant by my magic. My relationship with my people and my regard for them was a factor in them saying "yes" to getting up at 2:30 a.m. I called my top five people and they all said "yes." However, they also said that they had gotten a call from the manager, and the only reason they were coming in at 3:00 a.m. was because I had asked them. UPS taught me how to be a good leader even when my leadership style conflicted with that of the company.

In summary, a good leader understands authority. A good leader understands submission. A good leader walks in humility. A good leader walks in love and has a high regard for their people. A good leader speaks the truth with love for those whom are entrusted to his care. A good leader leads with love. A good leader builds relationships with their people and takes care of them.

In God's Kingdom here on earth, there are ranks of authority not ranks of superiority. This should be true for all organizations. There must be ranks of authority for things to get accomplished in any organization. In the Old Testament we read about how Moses was judging the people of Israel after they came out Egypt. Exodus 18:13-26:

13 The next day Moses took his seat to serve as judge for the people, and they stood around him from morning till evening. 14 When his father-in-law saw all that Moses was doing for the people, he said, What is this you are doing for the people? Why do you alone sit as judge, while all these people stand around you from morning till evening?" 15 Moses answered him, "Because the people come to me to seek God's will. 16 Whenever they have a dispute, it is brought to me, and I decide between the parties and inform them of God's decrees and instructions." 17 Moses' father-in-law replied, "What you are doing is not good. 18 You and these people who come to you will only wear yourselves out. The work is too heavy for you; you cannot handle it alone. 19 Listen now to me and I will give you some advice, and may God be with you. You must be the people's representative before God and bring their disputes to him. 20 Teach them his decrees and instructions and show them the way they are to live and how they are to behave. 21 But select capable men from all the people— men who fear God, trustworthy men who hate dishonest gain—and appoint them as officials over thousands, hundreds, fifties, and tens. 22 Have them always serve as judges for the people but have them bring every difficult case to you; the simple cases they can decide themselves. That will make your load lighter because they will share it with you. 23 If you do this and God so commands, you will be able to stand the strain, and all these people will go home satisfied."24 Moses listened to his father-in-law and did everything he said. 25 He chose capable men from all Israel and made them leaders of the people, officials over thousands, hundreds, fifties, and tens. 26 They always served as judges for the people.

This passage shows how Moses set up the lines of authority in the nation of Israel for judging and deciding matters that arose among the people. Verse 25 calls them leaders. Moses established a 'Chain of Command' to help deal with the issues that arose. Interestingly, Moses's father-in-law, Jethro, was a priest of Midian. Midian was the fourth son of Abraham the patriarch. It follows that Abraham would have instructed his sons in the ways of Jehovah. The Bible does not tell us the god that Jethro served as a priest, but it does say in Exodus 18:10-11, that Jethro believed that the Lord was greater than all the other gods. This seemed to be a common thread in the Bible at that time. Jehovah is just one of the gods. Later, we learn from the Scripture that there is only Jehovah and all other gods are idols of wood, stone, clay or gold.

Psalms 135: 14-18 reads:

14 *For the Lord will judge His people And will have compassion on His servants.*

15 The idols of the nations are but silver and gold, The work of man's hands.

16 They have mouths, but they do not speak; They have eyes, but they do not see;

17 They have ears, but they do not hear, Nor is there any breath at all in their mouths.

18 Those who make them will be like them, Yes, everyone who trusts in them.

So why do the Nations around Israel serve and believe in these 'gods? 1 Corinthians 10:13-22:

13 No temptation has overtaken you, but such as is common to man; and God is faithful, who will not allow you to be tempted beyond what you are able, but with the temptation will provide the way of escape also, so that you will be able to endure it. 14 Therefore, my beloved, flee from idolatry. 15 I speak as to wise men; you judge what I say. 16 Is not the cup of blessing which we bless a sharing in the blood of Christ? Is not the bread which we break a sharing in the body of Christ? 17 Since there is one bread, we who are many are one body; for we all partake of the one bread. 18 Look at the nation Israel; are not those who eat the sacrifices sharers in the altar? 19 What do I mean then? That a thing sacrificed to idols is anything, or that an idol is anything? 20 No, but I say that the things which the Gentiles sacrifice, they sacrifice to demons and not to God; and I do not want you to become sharers in demons. 21 You cannot drink the cup of the Lord and the cup of demons; you cannot partake of the table of the Lord and the table of demons. 22 Or do we provoke the Lord to jealousy? We are not stronger than He, are we?

2 Timothy 4:1-3 :

1 But the Spirit explicitly says that in later times some will fall away from the faith, paying attention to deceitful spirits and doctrines of demons, 2 by means of the hypocrisy of liars seared in their own conscience as with a branding iron, 3 men who forbid marriage and advocate abstaining from foods which God has created to be gratefully shared in by those who believe and know the truth.

The nations of the land of Canaan and the nations of today serve these idols because the demons behind these idols are real. These demons can speak and influence and draw people away from the One True God. What does this have to do with the divine tension of leadership? Even God, who is superior in every way to all that He has created, does not force His leadership upon us. He gently woos us and asks us to trust Him and follow His leadership. Not because it is what is best for Him, but because it is what is best for us. This is another quality of a good leader. A good leader, out of love, desires what is best for those they lead. That includes discipline. Even discipline and correction should be done in love and out of desire for what is best for those we lead. Hebrews 12:5: *"My son, do not regard lightly the discipline of the Lord, Nor faint when you are reproved by Him; 6 For those whom the Lord loves He disciplines, And He scourges every son whom He receives." 7 It is for discipline that you endure; God deals with you as with sons; for what son is there whom his father does not discipline? 8 But if you are without discipline, of which all have become partakers, then you are illegitimate children and not sons. 9 Furthermore, we had earthly fathers to discipline us, and we respected them; shall we not much rather be subject to the Father of spirits, and live? 10 For they disciplined us for a short time as seemed best to them, **but He disciplines us for our good**, so that we may share His holiness. 11 All discipline for the moment seems not to be joyful, but sorrowful; **yet to those who have been trained by it, afterwards it yields the peaceful fruit of righteousness.***

There are designated lines of authority not designated lines of superiority in the Kingdom of God here on earth. In the rest of creation different principles apply, and we are less in superiority to the Angels of God. Psalms 8:3-6 reads:

3 When I consider Your heavens, the work of Your fingers, The moon and the stars, which You have ordained; 4 What is man that You take thought of him, And the son of man that You care for him? 5 Yet You have made him a little lower than God, And You crown him with glory and majesty! 6 You make him to rule over the works of Your hands; You have put all things under his feet,

Hebrews 2:5-9 reads:

5 For He did not subject to angels the world to come, concerning which we are speaking. 6 But one has testified somewhere, saying, "What is man, that You remember him? Or the son of man, that You are concerned about him? 7 "You have made him for a little while lower than the angels; You have crowned him with glory and honor, And have appointed him over the works of Your hands; 8 You have put all things in subjection under his feet. "For in subjecting all things to him, He left nothing that is not subject to him. But now we do not yet see all things subjected to him. 9 But we do see Him who was made for a little while lower than the angels, namely, Jesus, because of the suffering of death crowned with glory and honor, so that by the grace of God He might taste death for everyone.

These verses make it clear that humanity is lower than the angels, and even Jesus in His humanity was 'lower' than the angels. The angels are superior to us in some created way even if that way is only a different form of life. The angels being fully spirit beings and us being a combination of spirit and physical beings. Humanity, however, does not have superiority one over the other. We are all created equal. Having said that, God has established an order of authority among humans. Designated lines of authority that we should see and respect. In the home those start with the father, then mother, finally children. Outside the home, there are slightly different lines of authority in the various institutions of humanity. There are lines of entity authority, such as companies and organizations. The United States Constitution gives equal authority to the government and to churches. One is not superior to the other. There are different lines of authority in governments starting with local government on up to federal governments. There are lines of military authority. We know what these lines are and should respect these lines, but they are not lines of superiority. No human is superior to any other human in all the ways that matter before God as our Creator.

SUBMISSION

What is submission? There are many variances to understanding this word. There are many emotions centered in this word. Too often submission in Scripture has been used like a club to get people to submit in various ways. When we come to the biblical idea of submission, we need to understand how it works in the kingdom of God. Does

God expect submission from us to Him as believers? If we choose not to submit does God force us to submit? Does He use His power and authority to beat us into submission? I think that we all know the answers to these questions. Does God bring correction to His children? Does that correction carry some form of pain? Hebrews 12:3-11, again reads:

3 For consider Him who has endured such hostility by sinners against Himself, so that you will not grow weary and lose heart. 4 You have not yet resisted to the point of shedding blood in your striving against sin; 5 and you have forgotten the exhortation which is addressed to you as sons, "My son, do not regard lightly the discipline of the Lord, Nor faint when you are reproved by Him; 6 For those whom the Lord loves He disciplines, And He scourges every son whom He receives." 7 It is for discipline that you endure; God deals with you as with sons; for what son is there whom his father does not discipline? 8 But if you are without discipline, of which all have become partakers, then you are illegitimate children and not sons. 9 Furthermore, we had earthly fathers to discipline us, and we respected them; shall we not much rather be subject to the Father of spirits, and live? 10 For they disciplined us for a short time as seemed best to them, but He disciplines us for our good, so that we may share His holiness. 11 All discipline for the moment seems not to be joyful, but sorrowful; yet to those who have been trained by it, afterwards it yields the peaceful fruit of righteousness.

Does God then discipline for us to submit? Is this a form

of 'forced submission? Often, we fail to understand things from God's perspective and so interpret events incorrectly. We see commands and correction as fences keeping us from fun rather than guard rails to keep us from harm. If a two-year-old child is drawn to an open fire while the parents are making S'mores, would a loving parent allow them to try to touch the flame or the hot coals? Of course not, and the answer is because they want to spare the child the pain and possibly, a life-long scar. If the child persists, and the parents bring some form of discipline, is the parent then a horrible parent if the child thinks that they are for not letting them touch what is hot? What is really happening then? There is immaturity on the part of the child. The parents, being more mature and wise, choose temporary discipline and correction to prevent what could be agonizing pain and permeant scarring. Will the child eventually gain understanding and be grateful for the loving discipline of the parents? Hopefully. Have we as believers found this to be true in our relationship with our Parent, God? Hopefully, we have discovered what Hebrews talks about in Chapter 12. Hopefully, we also learn to submit to the loving commands and direction of our Father understanding that it is what is best for us. This is loving submission. We submit to God out of love because we understand that we do not see as He sees. We do not understand as He understands. We recognize our limitations and the infinite capacity of our God. Hopefully, once we mature enough to understand God's nature, we do lovingly submit to His authority even when we may not understand the why's. In the home, or the nuclear family, God has designed the man to be the lead. Men are created by God to be in this position. Does that mean women cannot lead at all? No, of course not, however, in the family, God has designed the man to lead.

We also need to understand that the marriage of a man and a woman reflects the relationship that the Godhead has with each other. The Godhead of Father, Son, and Holy Spirit is a relationship of oneness. The marriage relationship is a relationship of oneness. The Godhead has a singular purpose in all that they do, there is no fraction or disagreement. They are one in spirit, purpose, movement, planning, execution, essence, thought and being. They are one in ways that are not listed here. This is the design that God has purposed for marriage. God designed the husband to - lovingly lead his wife - to protect and provide. I often walk slightly ahead of my wife when we are out and about. I do not do this as some misogynistic display of my superiority to her as a woman. I do it to watch out for her, to protect her, to be the first in the line of possible danger, as a loving way to lay down my life for her. I hope I understand, by the example of Jesus, that this is the way a husband should treat his wife. He should go first, that is what Jesus did for His bride. He went to the cross first so she would not have to go to the cross. He came to bring her everything and his life, death and resurrection accomplished that for her.

Now, in this time, I get to be Jesus to my wife. I get to love her unconditionally, to sacrifice for her, lay down my life and my dreams for her. I get to help her become all that she has destined by God to become. When husbands are Jesus to their wives it becomes easy to submit to his loving leadership. The 'S' word is not a curse word but a blessing from God that brings order, union and oneness. But submission goes far beyond the nuclear family, it extends out to all relationships, entities, companies, militaries, and governments. Often there are consequences for rebellion against designated lines of authority. I have to do my work when I am hired by a company, or I can be fired. I may offer to volunteer for a worthy cause, but if I do nothing then I may be asked to leave and not return. I may choose to not follow the orders of my officer which may land me in involuntary P.E. or even the brig. We also have the choice of obedience to God, and when we choose to willfully disobey, we reap what we sow. The life of David is an example of the consequence of wrong and destructive choices. Do we have to learn obedience and submission? Yes, Jesus had to learn that as well. Hebrews 5:7-9, reads of Jesus:

7 Who in the days of his flesh, when he had offered up prayers and supplications with strong crying and tears unto him that was able to save him from death, and was heard in that he feared; 8 Though he were a Son, yet learned he obedience by the things which he suffered; 9 And being made perfect, he became the author of eternal salvation unto all them that obey him;

Jesus learned obedience by all that He suffered. His

suffering was the pathway to obedience, submission, and trust even in the greatest trial Jesus ever faced in the Garden of Gethsemane. In all those trials and temptations, throughout His whole life, Jesus had to submit to the will of the Father and trust. Was it easy for Jesus to submit? We see, as adults, that it seemed easy. The Garden of Gethsemane was the place where the submission was the most difficult for Jesus. He prayed over and over that God the Father's will would be done even as He asked for the cup of suffering to pass from Him. I wonder if submission was as easy as we think it was when we look at the gospels and see Jesus mostly as an adult. Hebrews 5:8 says that *Jesus learned obedience by the things that He suffered.* I don't think that this applies only to his torment in the Garden of Gethsemane. John Paul Jackson taught a Scriptural and Godly principle that your small private victories over darkness establishes a pattern for large public victories over darkness.

Is it possible to face a large-scale public trial if you have not built a pattern of submission and trust with God in the small trials of our personal lives? Look at 1 Samuel 17:33-37: David said to Saul: *"Let no one lose heart on account of this Philistine; your servant will go and fight him." 33 Saul replied, "You are not able to go out against this Philistine and fight him; you are only a young man, and he has been a warrior from his youth." 34 But David said to Saul, "Your servant has been keeping his father's sheep. When a lion or a bear came and carried off a sheep from the flock, 35 I went after it, struck it and rescued the sheep from its mouth. When it turned on me, I seized it by its hair, struck it and killed it. 36 Your servant has killed both the lion and the bear; this uncircumcised Philistine will be like one of them, because he has defied the armies of the living God. 37 The Lord who rescued me from the paw of the lion and the paw of the bear will rescue me from the hand of this Philistine."*

David faced many battles protecting the sheep. He mentions two larger battles, but surely there were many smaller ones as well. David never mentions wolves, snakes, or smaller predatory mammals that may kill sheep or lambs. But for sure David protected the sheep over the years from more than one lion and one bear attack. It was all these private victories where David submitted to and trusted the Lord, and those victories gave him confidence to face Goliath. Jesus had Goliath moments in his forty days of temptations by the devil and the Goliath of Gethsemane. He struggled, but He still submitted and trusted. Of course, trust is another necessary attribute of submission. Think about it. If you know the person asking you to do something different or even difficult, are you not more likely to submit to the task if you are convinced that they love you and are worthy of your trust? Jesus learned obedience for sure, but isn't obedience really submission to the will of another? We do not like to submit. One reason is that we are overly independent in our culture, and no one is going to tell us 'we have to' do anything. Some of this, probably the great majority, is fallen human nature, but some is culture. Secondly, we have a difficult time trusting others to do anything for us.

I heard a story about a basketball player who began to do evangelistic work and used basketball to illustrate some of the truths of the Gospel. He was an amazing free throw shooter and could repeatedly make fifty free throws in a row. He would challenge others to do the same, but no one would be able to do fifty in a row. He next challenged his audience to do it like their life depended on it. When there was failure to complete the tasks, and therefore save their lives, he then said to the others left that he would shoot the fifty free throws for them. When he asked the group who did not want him to shoot for them, he was always surprised by so many raising their hands. In one session he asked the question, and an older woman raised her hand. She admitted that there was no way possible she could make the fifty free throws in a row. When he asked her if she thought that he could do it for her she admitted that he most likely could because she had seen him shoot the fifty in a row several times. He then asked why she would not let him shoot for her. She said that there was no way she was trusting her life into the hands of another. This story illustrates our stubborn, sinful independence and self-will that can also affect our submission to Jesus as Savior and especially Lord. But it also illustrates our independence to all other authority and our difficulties submitting to authority. How do we strike a balance here in our lives between independency and submission, as well as between leading and following?

Following the example of Jesus is a good place to start. Jesus was totally submitted to the will of His Father and the direction of the Holy Spirit while he walked among people. He was also one of the greatest leaders that the world has ever seen. Jesus demonstrated servant leadership in His earthly mission as our Savior. His life's work has affected the lives of millions even if they were not believers in 'The Way.' Jesus balanced perfectly on the tightrope of submission and leadership. Studying His life will help us to balance this issue as well.

CHAPTER SIX

Was Peter the First Pope? The Balance of Revelation and Knowledge

There is a contention between the Catholic Church and most other churches about something called apostolic secession. We will discuss this here because the contention is the point that illustrates why there is a divine tension and subsequence balance between revelation and knowledge. Apostolic succession is a doctrine of the Roman Catholic Church that gives the current pope the apostolic authority that many believe that the apostles had in the New Testament. The Catholics believe that they can trace an unbroken line of apostolic succession all the way back to the Apostle Peter, who they claim was the first pope of the Roman church. This is important to the Catholic church because they believe that it gives the popes the authority to write Scripture and their writings to be infallible. Many non-Catholics believe that their basis for believing apostolic succession is sketchy. Some of the early church fathers disagreed with the beginnings of this push toward apostolic succession. One was Justin Martyr, (100-165

AD) who wrote, 'The rock upon which Christ will build His church means the faith of testimony.' Another example is church historian, Eusebius, who also wrote: "The brother of the Lord, James, took over leadership of the church with the apostles when control passed to them." Non-Catholics looking back find the early stages of papacy in the fact that Rome was the capitol of the Roman Empire.

Dr. David F. Wells, a research professor at Gordon-Conwell Theological Seminary and author, writes:

> *It is, in fact, more plausible to think that the emergence of the Roman pontiff to power and prominence happened by natural circumstance rather than divine appointment. This took place in two stages. First, it was the church in Rome that emerged to prominence and only then, as part of its eminence, did its leader begin to stand out. The Catholic church has inverted these facts by suggesting that apostolic power and authority, indeed, Peter's preeminent power and authority, established the Roman bishop whereas, in fact, the Roman bishopric's growing ecclesiastical prestige derived, not from Peter, but from the church in Rome (8).*

> *Dr. Wells goes on to explain that the church, in several councils, expressly condemned the attempts of the papacy to assert universal authority and jurisdiction.*

Cyprian, in northern Africa, argued that the words, "You are Peter …" were not a charter for the papacy, but in fact applied to all bishops. Furthermore, at the third Council of Carthage in 256, he asserted that the Roman bishop should not attempt to be a "bishop of bishops" and exercise "tyrannical" powers.

Wells explains the gradual development of the false claims of the bishop of Rome and the forces that gave them the power to be asserted. Not surprisingly, much of this comes from the church's all too close relationship with secular government (8).

Emperor Constantine, prior to a pivotal battle, saw a vision and turned to Christianity. The church, which had lived a lonely existence on the "outside" up to this time, now enjoyed an unexpected imperial embrace. As a result, from this point on, the distinction between appropriate ecclesiastical demeanor and worldly pretensions to pomp and power were increasingly lost. In the Middle Ages, the distinction disappeared entirely. In the sixth century, Pope Gregory brazenly exploited this by asserting that the "care of the whole church" had been placed in the hands of Peter and his successors in Rome (9).

This is a brief background to give a little context to a passage of Scripture found in Matthew 16:13-20, which reads:

13 Now when Jesus came into the district of Caesarea Philippi, He was asking His disciples, "Who do people say that the Son of Man is?" 14 And they said, "Some say John the Baptist; and others, Elijah; but still others, Jeremiah, or one of the prophets." 15 He said to them, "But who do you say that I am?" 16 Simon Peter answered, "You are the Christ, the Son of the living God." 17 And Jesus said to him, "Blessed are you, Simon Barjona, because flesh and blood did not reveal this to you, but My Father who is in heaven. 18 I also say to you that you are Peter, and upon this rock I will build My church; and the gates of Hades will not overpower it. 19 I will give you the keys of the kingdom of heaven; and whatever you bind on earth shall have been bound in heaven, and whatever you loose on earth shall have been loosed in heaven." 20 Then He warned the disciples that they should tell no one that He was the Christ.

This passage is the key passage that the Catholics and non-Catholics use as proof text for Peter either being or not being the first pope. The reason that the Catholics use it seems kind of obvious if Peter was indeed the first pope. The reason that the non-Catholics use this passage is that the word for Peter in the Greek and rock in the Greek are two different words. Peter is from the Greek , *Πέτρος* Pétros, pet'-ros; apparently a primary word; a (piece of) rock; as a name, Petrus, an apostle:—Peter, rock. Rock is the Greek word, $\pi\acute{\epsilon}\tau\rho\alpha$ pétra, pet'-ra; a (mass of) rock (literally or figuratively):—rock. So, non-Catholics say that Peter means small stone, which can be implied from the translation, and Petra means mass of rock or, 'bedrock.'

I believe that Jesus was not referring to Peter or Himself when he said, 'upon this rock.' I believe He was referring to the revelation that Peter had received, and Jesus confirmed when He said, 'flesh and blood has not revealed this to you but my Father in heaven.' Almost all the writers I have read think that Jesus was referring to either Peter or Himself. There was only one writer I could find that says something different, and that was Justin Martyr, who said, 'The rock upon which Christ will build His church means the faith of testimony.' I am sure that there can be more research done in this area. When I look at other passages of Scripture, in conjunction with Matthew 16, I am even more inclined to stand where I stand on revelation being the 'rock'. When you look at the other passages in the New Testament that talk about binding and loosing, which is also in Matthew 18, you discover that the context is different. This is important because if Matthew 16 is all about Peter why does Jesus say the same thing to all the disciples in Matthew 18? The other non-Catholic piece I question based on Scripture is what Paul says in the epistles about foundation and building the church. Paul says that, *'No foundation can any man lay except that which is laid which is Christ Jesus.'* 1 Corinthians 3:11. Paul goes on to say that the foundation of the church is the apostle and prophets in Ephesians 2:19-22:

19 So then you are no longer strangers and aliens, but you are fellow citizens with the saints, and are of God's household, 20 having been built on the foundation of the apostles and prophets, Christ Jesus Himself being the corner stone, 21 in whom the whole building, being fitted together, is growing into a holy temple in the Lord, 22 in whom you also are being built together into a dwelling of God in the Spirit.

There are many verses that refer to Jesus as the foundational cornerstone, Romans 9:23: '*Just as it is written, "Behold, I lay in Zion a stone of stumbling and a rock of offense, and he who believes in Him will not be disappointed."* Isaiah 28:16, *Therefore thus says the Lord God, "Behold, I am laying in Zion a stone, a tested stone, a costly cornerstone for the foundation, firmly placed. He who believes in it will not be disturbed.* 1 Peter 2:4-8, *And coming to Him as to a living stone which has been rejected by men but is choice and precious in the sight of God, you also, as living stones, are being built up as a spiritual house for a holy priesthood, to offer up spiritual sacrifices acceptable to God through Jesus Christ. For this is contained in Scripture: "Behold, I lay in Zion a choice stone, a precious corner stone, and he who believes in Him will not be disappointed. "This precious value, then, is for you who believe; but for those who disbelieve, the stone which the builders rejected, this became the very corner stone, a stone of stumbling and a rock of offense"; for they stumble because they are disobedient to the word, and to this doom they were also appointed.*

Acts 4:10-12, Let *it be known to all of you and to all the people of Israel, that by the name of Jesus Christ the Nazarene, whom you crucified, whom God raised from the dead—by this name this man stands here before you in good health. He is the stone, which was rejected by you, the builders, but which became the chief corner stone. And there is salvation in no one else; for there is no other name under heaven that has been given among men by which we must be saved."* Psalms 118:22, *The stone which the builders rejected Has become the chief corner stone.*

All these verses are focused on Jesus being the chief cornerstone. While the chief cornerstone is part of the foundation it is not the whole foundation. New Studio Architecture writes of a cornerstone: 'In relation to architecture, a cornerstone is traditionally the first stone laid for a structure, with all other stones laid in reference. A cornerstone marks the geographical location by orienting a building in a specific direction.' (9)

Most cornerstones, before the 19th century, were laid in things like cathedrals and major structures and especially in structures that had some type of significance. Since the cornerstone was the stone that gave direction to all other stones in the foundation it was the most important stone. Cornerstones were placed in alignment with celestial bodies or in a northeastern position, on purpose, to give a directional quality to the whole building. You can see why Jesus is called the cornerstone of the church. In the universal church and the local church. He is the one that gives direction to the rest of the structure. Another analogy is Jesus as the head of the church for the same reason. However, we also see that Jesus being the chief cornerstone is not the whole foundation. That is why Paul says that the foundation of the church is the Apostle and Prophet.

Galatians 2:20 reads: *And are built upon the foundation of the apostles and prophets, Jesus Christ himself being the chief cornerstone.* Some other verses that mention foundations are, Romans 15:20, *Yea, so have I strived to preach the gospel, not where Christ was named, lest I should build upon another man's foundation,* and 1 Corinthians 3:10, *According to the grace of God which is given unto me, as a wise master builder, I have laid the foundation, and another builds thereon. But let every man take heed how he builds thereupon.* These verses lay out that when Paul talks about foundation, he includes others and not just Christ alone. There is an aspect of the church's foundation that is in Christ alone which is why Paul writes in 1 Corinthians 3:10: *For no man can lay a foundation other than the one which is laid, which is Jesus Christ.* The foundation of the new covenant and the Gospel is Jesus. His death, burial, and resurrection are the foundational tenants of the Christian faith.

What does this have to do with Peter? From this

vantage point we can see that Peter is not the foundation of the church or the first pope as the Catholic's declare. However, understanding what Paul says about the apostle and prophets gives us a clue to understanding the other aspects of the foundation. The apostles and prophets were the two called offices that brought revelation to the church. Sometimes as a whole, which is seen in the New Testament writings. and sometimes they brought revelation to specific churches. Paul's letters were written to specific churches but have a universal application to all churches. When a new church is started there needs to be revelation for the beginning of the church. What is the church's location and purpose in that location beyond the obvious of people being saved? Who are the leaders and elders to be, and how are they chosen? What is the vision or specific mission to be? These are all foundational questions that need revelation to be answered. So, when we look at Jesus's declaration to Peter about the revelation given to him as being the foundation upon which the church will be built, it makes more sense then that Peter was not the rock or foundation of the church. What does any of this have to do with divine tension or the mystery of balance? A clue to that answer is given in 1 Corinthians 13:8-12:

8 Love never fails; but if there are gifts of prophecy, they will be done away; if there are tongues, they will cease; if there is knowledge, it will be done away. 9 For we know in part and we prophesy in part; 10 but when the perfect comes, the partial will be done away. 11 When I was a child, I used to speak like a child, think like a child, reason like a child; when I became a man, I did away with childish things. 12 For now we see in a mirror dimly, but then face to face; now I know in part, but then I will know fully just as I also have been fully known.

There is more in these verses than we should try to tackle in this book about balance. Suffice to say that Paul was not talking about the completion of the Canon when he writes about the perfect coming. None of the early church fathers believed he was talking about the 'Canon.' When you read this in context it points to two possibilities which will eventually be reality for all believers. Firstly, the perfection or completion that comes with death and being absent from the body to be present with the Lord (2 Corinthians 5:8), or secondly, the perfection or completion that comes with Jesus's return. Looking at verses 9 and 10 we see the application to the balance between revelation and knowledge. This is a divine tension that exists in the church specifically for humility and relationship. The church needs the Old Testament and the New Testament as the foundational, written, declaration of the Word of God. However, the church also needs current and specific revelation to function well in the here and now. As an example: As a believer, I know - based on the teaching in Scripture, that I was to marry someone of like-faith. My problem was that I knew many eligible young ladies who were believers. My dilemma was which one of these ladies God had chosen for me as my spouse? Do I just hunt, and peck, and choose based on some physical and fleeting aspect? Do I choose to not look and just wait until God drops this lady in my lap and suddenly, I know? Or do I seek God, and ask Him to direct me to the one person who He has chosen to be my wife? When I was younger, I did not understand these principles as well as I do now, and I was taught that God no longer communicates to us in any way except the Scriptures. However, that has never been my reality. God has always communicated with me through the inner voice of the Holy Spirit since I was saved at age fifteen. Back then, before I was taught differently, I just believed that this was the way things worked as a Christian.

Since then, God has taught me many things and this subject is one that He has helped me to understand more clearly. God has corrected me many times on my interpretation and understanding of His Scripture, and I was always reminded when He did this of what Paul said in II Corinthians 4:2: *But we have renounced the things hidden because of shame, not walking in craftiness or adulterating the word of God, but by the manifestation of truth commending ourselves to every man's conscience in the sight of God.* This is the part of revelation that produces humility in the believer. Why? Because the Scripture clearly pronounces in 1 Corinthians 8: 1-3: *Now concerning things sacrificed to idols, we know that we all have knowledge. Knowledge makes arrogant, but love edifies. 2 If anyone supposes that he knows anything, he has not yet known as he ought to know; 3 but if anyone loves God, he is known by*

Him. This is the truth - knowledge alone makes arrogance. This was the problem with the Pharisees and Jesus in the Gospels. The Pharisees thought they knew, and no one could tell them different. There's a non-Scriptural proverb that says, "There is no one so blind as the one who refuses to see and no one so deaf as the one who refuses to listen." Didn't Jesus say often, "He who has ears to hear and eyes to see…" and did he not call the Pharisees blind? This is the tension that balances revelation and knowledge. Paul brings the two together in a balance when he writes: *15 For this reason I too, having heard of the faith in the Lord Jesus which exists among you and\your love for all the saints, 16 do not cease giving thanks for you, while making mention of you in my prayers; 17 that the God of our Lord Jesus Christ, the Father of glory,* ***may give to you a spirit of*** <u>***wisdom***</u> ***and of*** <u>***revelation***</u> ***in the*** <u>***knowledge of Him.***</u> *18 I pray that the eyes of your heart may be enlightened, so that you will know what is the hope of His calling, what are the riches of the glory of His inheritance in the saints, 19and what is the surpassing greatness of His power toward us who believe. Ephesians 1:15-18.*

The second aspect of relationship is plain as well in 1 Corinthians 13:9-12. Paul says that *he knows in part and prophecies in part.* He goes on to say that he sees dimly like looking in a mirror, which is a reference to revelation, but when perfection comes, he will see face to face and know fully as he is known by God. This is about relationship. Relationship must include communication and communing with one another. Think of it like this; Imagine a lady who meets her perfect man, and they know that they love each other so they get married quickly. On the wedding day after the ceremony, he tells his bride that he is leaving, and he will return someday but maybe not before she dies. He hands her sixty-six love letters he has written and tells her that everything she needs know, now and in the future, is in the love letters. Once he leaves, she will never see him again, she will never hear him again, and he will never write her new letters. All communication and communion will cease, and he expects her to be faithful since he has set her up with a house and money to survive. How long would it take for the average woman to grow concerned about the marriage relationship that she just stepped into? And how long would it be before she grew lonely and discouraged as a young bride? Would anyone say that this man cared about relationship with his spouse? Would anyone blame her if she sought relationship elsewhere maybe even after the years of waiting for him to be declared dead? If we being 'evil' would say that this is not a relationship, then would God consider it a relationship? And He cares about relationship more than us. Romans 5:8 reads: *But God demonstrates His own love toward us, in that while we were yet sinners, Christ died for us.* Why? For reconciliation of the relationship that was damaged by the fall in the Garden of Eden. The tension that exists between revelation and knowledge is balanced by humility and relationship.

CHAPTER SEVEN

Trials and Temptations: A Balance of Understanding

Are trials and temptations really something that needs to be kept in some kind of balance? Possibly. But if there is greater understanding of trials and temptations then maybe we can find a balance that plays out well in this life and our spiritual walk. Trials should be understood as an integral part of the Christian's life. However, trials do not just happen to believers alone. All people face trials of some kind over the course of their lives. Trials come for many and various reasons. We can also see them as tests. We can face tests or trials of endurance, and not all these are physical like running a marathon. We can face trials of patience, trials of relationship, trials of faithfulness, finances, resources, and family dynamics. There are many more that come to mind which I am sure you have thought about as you read this short list. The purpose here is to define and explain trials and temptations so we can strike a balance between the two.

TRIALS

Trials are something that as believers we often misunderstand. We do not see them as we should, and so we try to bear up under them rather than embrace them. We often hear about the patience of Job, who suffered greatly under several trials. Firstly, he lost all his possessions and wealth, secondly, he lost almost all his employees, and he lost all his children. Then Job lost his health. Even his wife was not supportive of his suffering, though we must realize that she was going through it as well. Lastly, and most importantly, in Job's situation, he lost his contact with God. We all have those moments when we feel like the heavens are brass, but imagine being Job, who was called blameless by God, feeling like the Heavens were brass. What we often miss in the story of Job is what the Scriptures say about him in the beginning. To help understand trials, let's go back there. The Scriptures declare that Job was the greatest in the east. After that, Scripture lists all his possessions and all his family. Scripture also tells us that Job was a righteous man, in fact, he was blameless! I wonder what God would say about us in a similar situation. Take Job, being who he was, and Heaven was silent to him. And he is not the only one in Scripture that felt that way. Look at Psalms 22:1-2: *1 My God, my God, why have You forsaken me? Far from my deliverance are the words of my groaning. 2 O my God, I cry by day, but You do not answer*; These words are also repeated by Jesus on the cross. We are in good company when we feel the heavens are silent. The next section is a scene in heaven where we see Satan coming before God with the other sons of God. God asks a question to which we know that He already knows the answer. What I find interesting is Satan's response about roaming around on the earth.

Here is how I see the confrontation with God by Satan. This is my poetic interpretation of the situation. Satan brags to God that he is the best runner in the earth. He is roaming. Immediately after Satan answers God, God talks about Job. This indicates that there is more to this situation than meets the eye because the challenge by Satan is met with God immediately talking about Job. This is what God says about Job: 1:8: *The Lord said to Satan, "Have you considered My servant Job? For there is no one like him on the earth, a blameless and upright man, fearing God and turning away from evil."* What I see is that when Satan brags about being the best runner, God tells him that Job can win any marathon. God says that Job is the best runner in all the earth and will even beat Satan in a race. What we see next is that Satan is the typical bully and must make sure that Job is hobbled before the race even begins. In chapter two, the scene in heaven repeats, and we see that in the race, Job, is way out in front. Now Satan does not just want to hobble Job, he wants to make him sick and break some bones, surely that will slow him down in the race. Satan then leaves, and the story shifts to center on what then happens with Job.

I need to interject a personal story here, so you understand where I get the poetic license in this story. I was out of the country and preparing a sermon to preach in a church that had invited me to speak. I felt led by the Lord to preach from the book of Job. As I was preparing my message, the summer Olympics were being televised, so I had the TV on to watch the gold rounds. I heard the announcer say that there was a race coming up, and I stopped what I was doing thinking it was going to be the gold round. When I got to the TV to watch, the announcer said that it was a trial round. I was disappointed because I wanted to watch the gold round not a trial round. As I headed back to my sermon, I felt the Holy Spirit nudge me about the type of round that was being raced. I thought trial round, trial round. Then it hit me, and I had my answer about trials that I had missed in all my reading and study before this point. I remember hearing messages about trials, and that they were to teach us something and that, therefore, we would enjoy trials. James even said that in James 1:2: *Consider it all joy, my brethren, when you encounter various trials.* I thought that this was such a contradiction. There is no way that people think trials are joyful. Then I came up with what I considered to be a clever spiritual answer.

I needed to understand what God wanted to teach me quickly so the trial would end, and I could get back to joy. Now studying Job and the trial he went through I realized that this was like an Olympic trial, except Job was actually in the gold round. How do athletes get to the Olympics? Well, they train and train and then they train some more, and they train to be perfect or as we may say, they train to be blameless in their performance. They train to get a perfect or blameless ten. During that training, where the coach is narrowing down the athletes for a trip to the Olympics, the athletes go through many trial rounds. Imagine if you were one of those athletes and you were working hard to be chosen for the Olympics. The coach announces that there is a trial coming up to see who will make the team. Would you say, "Forget it coach I never liked trials, so I don't want to suffer through another one." Or would you stand up to demonstrate that all your talent, hard work, and training will now show the coach that you can be a part of the team and maybe, just maybe, you get an opportunity to win the gold.

Suddenly, I realized why trials were to be counted all joy. It becomes an opportunity to demonstrate to the coach that you are ready for the event. The same is true for spiritual matters. God is our most ardent coach and cheerleader. If you listen to what God says about Job to Satan it is clear. He was not offering Job up to Satan, He was praising Job and telling Satan there was no way he (Satan) would win the race. Now that I had a better understanding of what the Father was doing, all the rest of the Scriptures about trials took on a new meaning. For the believer, the ultimate goal of trials is to bring us into the image of Jesus. Why? Because of what Jesus told Philip in John 14:7-11: 7 *If you really know me, you will know my Father as well. From now on, you do know him and have seen him." 8 Philip* *said, "Lord, show us the Father and that will be enough for us." 9 Jesus answered: "Don't you know me, Philip, even after I have been among you such a long time? **Anyone who has seen me has seen the Father.** How can you say, 'Show us the Father'? 10 Don't you believe that I am in the Father, and that the Father is in me? The words I say to you I do not speak on my own authority. Rather, it is the Father, living in me, who is doing his work. 11 Believe me when I say that I am in the Father and the Father is in me; or at least believe on the evidence of the works themselves.*

Jesus is the express image of the Father in living flesh. Knowing this it becomes understandable why God would want us to be like Jesus. Romans 8:28-29 says: *28 And we know that God causes all things to work together for good to those who love God, to those who are called according to His purpose. 29 For those whom He foreknew, He also predestined to become conformed to the image of His Son, so that He would be the firstborn among many brethren.*

Next Philippians 3:7-11 says: *7 But whatever things were gain to me, those things I have counted as loss for the sake of Christ. 8 More than that, I count all things to be loss in view of the surpassing value of knowing Christ Jesus my Lord, for whom I have suffered the loss of all things, and count them but rubbish so that I may gain Christ, 9 and may be found in Him, not having a righteousness of my own derived from the Law, but that which is through faith in Christ, the righteousness which comes from God on the basis of faith, 10 t**hat I may know Him and the power***

*of His resurrection and the fellowship of His sufferings,
being conformed to His death; 11 in order that I may attain
to the resurrection from the dead.* Paul understood that the
Father's purpose was to bring him into the image of Jesus.
Paul wanted to *know* Jesus, and that word know is t*o know
by experience through relationship.* Why is understanding
these Scriptures important? Because they help us to
understand the why of a trial and to understand that there
is an ultimate purpose in the trial. We are in training to be
like Jesus, and during that training there will be tests and
trials along the way as opportunities to demonstrate our
progress, not just to God, but to all those around whose
lives intersect with ours.

Now let's see how some other Scriptures fit into this
reality. The next passage is quite a few verses, but the
context is amazing when we see the part about trials. 1 Peter
1:3-9: *3 Blessed be the God and Father of our Lord Jesus
Christ, who according to His great mercy has caused us
to be born again to a living hope through the resurrection
of Jesus Christ from the dead, 4 to obtain an inheritance
which is imperishable and undefiled and will not fade
away, reserved in heaven for you, 5 who are protected by
the power of God through faith for a salvation ready to
be revealed in the last time. 6 In this you greatly rejoice,
even though now for a little while, if necessary, you have
been distressed by various trials, 7 so that the proof of your
faith, being more precious than gold which is perishable,
even though tested by fire, may be found to result in praise*

and glory and honor at the revelation of Jesus Christ; 8 and though you have not seen Him, you love Him, and though you do not see Him now, but believe in Him, you greatly rejoice with joy inexpressible and full of glory, 9 obtaining as the outcome of your faith the salvation of your souls.

Peter tells his readers the amazing salvation that they have through verse 5, and then he tells them that they could greatly rejoice in this salvation. Then he goes on to tell them that they may be experiencing difficult trials and even offers some reason as to why there are trials. What I find amazing here is when you fit these verses into the Olympic illustration, we see that the test is much more precious than gold, or a gold medal, and that winning the race or enduring the trial leads to *us* being praised by Jesus when He appears. For a moment, we get to take the platform and stand in the place as the gold winner. Now, the next verse is in James 1:2-4: *2 Consider it all joy, my brethren, when you encounter various trials, 3 knowing that the testing of your faith produces endurance. 4 And let endurance have its perfect result, so that you may be perfect and complete, lacking in nothing.* Now with a clearer understanding of the place and purpose for trials I see how I can count it joy to face them. God trusts me enough to put me in the trial, and I am excited to demonstrate that He has not chosen unwisely. I realize that He is my greatest Cheerleader. He wants me to succeed more than I want to succeed. I see the trials from a better and new perspective and find it joyous that God cares enough to improve my faith and demonstrates His faith in me by allowing the trial to take place.

TEMPTATIONS

Temptations are different than trials. Temptations come from some place other than God. James tells us in chapter 1:12-16: 12 *Blessed is a man who perseveres under trial; for once he has been approved, he will receive the crown of life which the Lord has promised to those who love Him. 13 Let no one say when he is tempted, "I am being tempted by God"; for God cannot be tempted by evil, and He Himself does not tempt anyone. 14 But each one is tempted when he is carried away and enticed by his own lust. 15 Then when lust has conceived, it gives birth to sin; and when sin is accomplished, it brings forth death. 16 Do not be deceived, my beloved brethren.*

One doctrinal resource lays out temptations from James in seven steps.

James describes a seven-step process:

1. Tempted.

This refers to a seed planted by the father of lies (John 8:44).

2. Drawn Away by Own Lusts.

The seed cannot conceive unless there is an egg with which to unite (Matthew 5:27-28).

3. Enticed.

This refers to the attraction of the two previous steps. To be enticed is "to be drawn on by exciting hope and desire."

4. Conception.

This is the joining of the seed and the egg to begin the germinating process (Job 15:35; Acts 5:4).

"They conceive trouble and bring forth futility; their womb prepares deceit." Job 15:35

"They conceive trouble and evil, and their hearts give birth only to deceit."–NLT.

While it remained, was it not your own? And after it was sold, was it not in your own.

control? Why have you conceived this thing in your heart? You have not lied to men but to God." Acts 5:4.

5. Formation.

This is the time before the eventual bringing forth when one is dwelling on it, mulling. it over in the mind and fantasizing about it. In essence, it is a time of feeding the conceived idea so that it grows stronger.

6. Birth/Bringing Forth.

> *This is the outward manifestation of that which to this point has only been inward (Psalms 7:14).*
>
> *Behold, the wicked brings forth iniquity; yes, he conceives trouble and brings forth falsehood. Psalms 7:14*

7. Death.

This is the final outcome of all temptation (Proverbs 16:25). All sin leads to tragic consequences.

There is a way that seems right to a man, but its end is the way of death. (11)

When we consider what James is saying and the layout of these seven steps, we can see that any issues connected to the evil one are not in the mix with this description of temptation. I believe that as believers the reason Satan is not in the mix is because we have the power from the Holy Spirit to resist temptation. Satan may be a part of temptations that come our way, but he only tries to tempt us in areas where we are weak. As an example, if I have an alcohol problem the alcohol offered to me may be a difficult temptation to which I am inclined to give in to during the temptation. If I never drink, and I am handed a drink by a friend at a party who tries to convince me it's okay to partake of the drink, it is easy for me to say no and refuse. What I believe James is saying is that no matter what we choose in a temptation, the choice as believers is our choice. When we stand before the Lord, we will not be able to say, "The devil made me do it." Does Satan tempt us? Of course, but he cannot force a believer to sin. 1 Corinthians 10:12-13 reads: *12 Therefore let him who thinks he stands take heed that he does not fall. 13 No temptation has overtaken you, but such as is common to man; and God is faithful, who will not allow you to be tempted beyond what you are able, but with the temptation will provide the way of escape also, so that you will be able to endure it.* Temptation may come, but if we learn to trust the Lord there is always a door of escape.

Jesus gives us some clues as to how to avoid temptation. He tells us in Matthew 6:13, as part of the Lord's prayer, *'And do not lead us into temptation, but deliver us from evil. For Yours is the kingdom and the power and the glory forever. Amen.'* Then he reminds the disciples in the Garden, *"Keep watching and praying that you may not enter into temptation; the spirit is willing, but the flesh is weak."* This is an interesting passage because Jesus had asked them to pray with Him, but they kept falling asleep. When you look at the passage in context, what was the temptation, and what was the weakness of the flesh? The weakness of the flesh is being tired, and the temptation is to give in to sleep when the Lord has asked us to pray with Him. Have you ever noticed that if you want to pray before bed, it seems very hard to stay awake? Too often we are in bed, and if you're like me, I fall asleep during my prayers.

This may be a time when the posture of prayer is important. If we were on our knees and it was uncomfortable, would that be enough of a catalyst to keep us awake during our prayer time? Probably. This may be a way for us to 'beat our bodies' as Paul says. This passage is not about hurting ourselves, it is about winning the battle with our flesh and beating the flesh. Like in a race, I beat my opponent to the finish line.

There is another interesting component to temptation. We are not always tempted by just our flesh. Sometimes, it is the enemy of our souls or one of his minions that tempts us. *Then Jesus was led up by the Spirit into the wilderness to be tempted by the devil.* Matthew 4:1. *...for forty days, being tempted by the devil. And He ate nothing during those days, and when they had ended, He became hungry.* Luke 4:2. *And He was in the wilderness forty days being tempted by Satan; and He was with the wild beasts, and the angels were ministering to Him.* Mark 1:13. *When the devil had finished every temptation, he left Him until an opportune time.* Luke 4:13. After Jesus finished all his testing and the temptations from the devil we read: *for we do not have a high priest who cannot sympathize with our weaknesses, but One who has been tempted in all things as we are, yet without sin.* Hebrews 4:15. Because He was tempted 'sorely' as the KJV calls it, *for since He Himself was tempted in that which He has suffered, He is able to come to the aid of those who are tempted.* Hebrews 2:18. Doesn't it help when we are suffering to have someone comfort us who has been through what we are going through? And doesn't it also help when we are trying to deal with the things in our past that haunt us, and there is someone who has gone through what we went through and comes along side to help? Jesus is both of those for us. Not only does He understand, but he feels our temptations and pain while we are going through it. He does not just minister to us, He, also, is with His Father and: *Therefore, He is able also to save forever those who draw near to God through Him, **since He always lives to make intercession for them**.* Hebrews 7:25. Jesus is praying and intercedes at the right hand of His Father in heaven for us in trials and temptations.

Another aspect of temptation that needs to be covered is found in Galatians: *Brethren, even if anyone is caught in any trespass, you who are spiritual, restore such a one in a spirit of gentleness; each one looking to yourself, so that you too will not be tempted.* Galatians 6:1. This temptation is provoked in us by the sin of someone else. When we help another in their attempt to overcome the sin they are caught in we need to be careful not to be tempted ourselves. The Greek word caught is, προλαμβάνω prolambánō, prol-am-ban'-o; from G4253: (πρό pró, pro; a primary preposition; "fore", i.e. in front of, prior (figuratively, superior) to:—above, ago, before, or ever), and G2983: (λαμβάνω lambánō, lam-ban'-o: to take),; to take in advance, i.e. (literally) eat before others have an opportunity; (figuratively) to anticipate, surprise:—come aforehand, overtake, take before. The meaning in this verse is that someone is taken before. It carries the idea of being taken by a sin before, like being caught off guard and then becoming entangled in the sin.

This aspect of trials and temptations is in addition to what may be considered the more 'normal' trials and temptation. Paul and Peter help us understand this type of temptation from a spirit realm vantage point when Paul tells us that we should not be unaware of the strategy of the evil one. The context is about confronting sin and then forgiving the sinner so that they experience love and comfort. Then Paul tells us, '*so that no advantage would be taken of us by Satan, for we are not ignorant of his schemes.*' 2 Corinthians 2:11. Paul then helps us to see that our warfare is not in the physical realm but the spirit realm. He writes about the spiritual armor that we have been given to fight a spirit battle. *10 Finally, be strong in the Lord and in the strength of His might. 11 Put on the full armor of God,* **so that you will be able to stand firm against the schemes of the devil.** *12 For our struggle is not against flesh and blood, but against the rulers, against the powers, against the world forces of this darkness, against the spiritual forces of wickedness in the heavenly places. 13 Therefore, take up the full armor of God, so that you will be able to resist in the evil day, and having done everything, to stand firm. 14 Stand firm therefore, having girded your loins with truth, and having put on the breastplate of righteousness, 15 and having shod your feet with the preparation of the gospel of peace; 16 in addition to all, taking up the shield of faith with which you will be able to extinguish all the flaming arrows of the evil one. 17 And take the helmet of salvation, and the sword of the Spirit, which is the word* *of God. 18 With all prayer and petition pray at all times in the Spirit, and with this in view, be on the alert with all perseverance and petition for all the saints,* Ephesians 6:10-18.

These verses are packed with information about spirit warfare that helps us do what Paul is telling us: to stand. Peter tells us, *8 Be of sober spirit, be on the alert. Your adversary, the devil, prowls around like a roaring lion, seeking someone to devour. 9 But resist him, firm in your faith, knowing that the same experiences of suffering are being accomplished by your brethren who are in the world.* 1 Peter 5:8-9.

As we wrap up this chapter and summarize, it becomes important to see the divine tension and balance in trials and temptations. We need to understand the difference so we can balance these out in our lives, but the divine tension is that God knows that we need trials and temptations to build our faith and make us stronger. The balance of this divine tension is our spiritual understanding of these truths. When we recognize that God works all these things for our good to bring us into the image of His Son, Jesus, it becomes easier for us to endure and stay faithful to God through the trials and temptations. Recognizing the difference and the spirit warfare of both is the tightrope we walk in the Spirit and the balance we need to stay above the fray.

CHAPTER EIGHT

Truth and Love: The Balance of Words and Actions

This is interesting because of the why of the chapter title. Truth almost always involves words, and love almost always involves actions. We struggle with this because we often do not know how to deliver truth in love because truth often comes across as harsh or judgmental. Why is truth harsh or judgmental? Because we do not like or want to change. We like our sin and our addictions, whatever they may be, and so we struggle against the truth, which if accepted, means we need to change. It is also important to recognize that we are not completely resistant to change. We like change if we think that it benefits us. We will accept radical change if it benefits us. How is this true? Because if we won the lottery for two hundred million, assuming we play the lottery, we would welcome the radical change to our lives that lots of money would bring. This type of radical change is a dark change because most people who win the lottery are ruined by it in a few years. The love of money is the root of all types of evil. As Paul says, and this type of change invites darkness, and humans love darkness rather than light because our deeds are evil. So back to the truth, we then think that we must prove our point of the truth with strong words and powerful arguments. But Paul tells us:

1 And when I came to you, brethren, I did not come with superiority of speech or of wisdom, proclaiming to you the testimony of God. 2 For I determined to know nothing among you except Jesus Christ, and Him crucified. 3 I was with you in weakness and in fear and in much trembling, 4 and my message and my preaching were not in persuasive words of wisdom, but in demonstration of the Spirit and of power, 5 so that your faith would not rest on the wisdom of men, but on the power of God. 1 Corinthians 2:1-5.

What is interesting and requires balance in the mystery of this chapter is, it is a piece of the upside-down Kingdom of God. If you haven't yet heard or recognized, the kingdom of God is upside down compared to the kingdoms of this world and certainly the 'kingdom' of the evil one. Jesus demonstrated this in His coming as a humble servant rather than a conquering king. What we need to see is that the things that we prize in our world are not what God prizes in His Kingdom. We prize strength, power and control. God prizes meekness, weakness, and submission. Look at this passage: *5 Let this mind be in you, which was also in Christ Jesus: 6 Who, being in the form of God, thought it not robbery to be equal with God: 7 But made himself of no reputation, and took upon him the form of a servant, and was made in the likeness of men: 8 And being found in fashion as a man, he humbled himself, and became obedient unto death, even the death of the cross. 9 Wherefore God also hath highly exalted him and given him a name which is above every name: 10 That at the name of Jesus every knee should bow, of things in heaven, and things in earth, and things under the earth; 11 And that every tongue should confess that Jesus Christ is Lord, to the glory of God the Father.* Philippians 2:5-11.

Think of it... God Almighty, in all His glory and splendor, humbled to the form of a lowly servant and in the likeness of humanity, just to die a horrible and disgraceful death. *6 You see, at just the right time, when we were still powerless, Christ died for the ungodly. 7 Very rarely will anyone die for a righteous person, though for a good person someone might possibly dare to die. 8 But God demonstrates his own love for us in this: While we were still sinners, Christ died for us.* Romans 5:6-8, This passage needs to be understood in conjunction with the Philippians passage. Jesus was not just a fellow human; He was God Incarnate. For understanding, God is not like us in any way, we may be like God, but He is not like us. God is as high above us as we are above the amoeba. The difference is that we are not some cute single celled creatures that swim in water. We are more like the cockroach that hides in the dark and lives off dead things such as sin. Remember these verses? *6 For all of us have become like one who is unclean, **and all our righteous deeds are like a filthy garment**; And all of* *us wither like a leaf, And our iniquities, like the wind, take us away. 7 There is no one who calls on Your name, Who arouses himself to take hold of You; For You have hidden Your face from us And have delivered us into the power of our iniquities.* Isaiah 64:6-7.

This Hebrew word for filthy carries the implication that the filthy cloth is a woman's menstrual cloth used during her period to absorb the flow. I'm sorry that this is graphic, however, this is how God sees our *good deeds*, not our evil ones. The illustration of the cockroach is pertinent because if we look at each other, as we often do, then we may say like Paul, *'though for a good person someone might possibly dare to die,'* but would we die for a cockroach? Something that we are far above in the creation of God. Does this offend our sense of who we are? Is our pride wounded because of this illustration? Understanding that our pride may be wounded or offended is part of grasping the vastness of the difference between the Living, Almighty God and us. Seeing this illustration gives us clarity about the humbling that Jesus went through for us. Were we worth it? Of course, because God loves us even if we don't love other parts of His creation, like cockroaches. Why is this important here? Because it demonstrates the upside downness of the Kingdom of God. It shows us how Jesus is willing to humble Himself and why this characteristic is so highly prized by God. Jesus being willing to humble Himself is why God has highly exulted Him. (Look back at Philippians 2 above)

Now what does this have to do with this chapter? Speaking the truth in love is also upside down. Or, as we could also say, it is counter intuitive. God's ways are counter intuitive to the ways of our sinful flesh. God says weak is strong, poor is rich, humble is exulted, love is a conqueror and meekness is strength. We see the opposite in the world, that's what we believe is the truth rather than what God says in His Word.

You have heard it said that actions speak louder than words, or walk the walk, don't just talk the talk. How do we find the balance in the tension between these two things? Can we speak the truth in love? What is interesting in the world today is the muddy waters around the word truth. I have my truth and you have your truth and everyone else has their truth, and no one really knows what the truth is anymore. Even the 'god' of science keeps changing the 'truth.' This is not a new thing in our current age because Pilate asked Jesus, 'what is truth?' two thousand years ago. For the believer it is not our responsibility to convince anyone of the truth, prove the truth, or even drag them into accepting the truth like a lawyer in the court room. Our responsibility is to communicate the truth, and then it is up to the Holy Spirit to convince and convict. He is the Spirit of truth, He does the convincing: 26 *"When the Helper comes, whom I will send to you from the Father, that is the Spirit of truth who proceeds from the Father, He will testify about Me.* John 15:26, 7 *But I tell you the truth, it is to your advantage that I go away; for if I do not go away, the Helper will not come to you; but if I go, I will send Him to you. 8 And He, when He comes, will convict the world concerning sin and righteousness and judgment; 9 concerning sin, because they do not believe in Me; 10 and concerning righteousness, because I go to the Father and you no longer see Me; 11 and concerning judgment, because the ruler of this world has been judged. 12 "I have many more things to say to you, but you cannot bear them now. 13 But when He, the Spirit of truth, comes, He will guide you into all the truth;* John 16:7-13.

But to communicate the truth we must know the truth which is why Jesus said that the Spirit of Truth will lead us into all truth. Submission is necessary to be led - submission to the Holy Spirit. What is also needed is humility, and didn't we just read that God highly prizes that quality in us? Why is humility needed? Because God first wants the truth to change us, and humility allows us to see the truth without our pride refusing to accept and change. Interestingly, God only wants what is best for us, and Romans 12 tells us if we humble ourselves and accept God's best then our lives will prove that it really is what is best for us and everyone else. *1 Therefore I urge you, brethren, by the mercies of God, to present your bodies a living and holy sacrifice, acceptable to God, which is your spiritual service of worship. 2 And do not be conformed to this world, but be transformed by the renewing of your mind, so that you may prove what the will of God is, that which is good and acceptable and perfect.* Romans 12:1-2.

Some of this boils down to whether or not we trust God. If we really know Him and trust Him then we realize that He only wants what is best for us, it is easier to submit to the process and allow the Spirit-led change in our lives. Then our lives reflect that change, and people see the walk that we have before them. This is the love part. Love changes our walk, and people can see that we are different. Maybe that is why Jesus told the disciples: *34 A new commandment I give to you, that you love one another, even as I have loved you, that you also love one another. 35 By this all men will know that you are My disciples, if you have love for one another."* John 13:34-35 Radical, God inspired love that first changes us and then affects those around us. If we have any doubt about love remember, *love never fails.* 1 Corinthians 13:8.

The way to balance this divine tension is to lead with love and walk in truth. We need to reach for love first. The movie, *Remember the Titans,* gives us some great insight into radical love and humility. Gerry Bertier and Julius Campbell were enemies in the beginning of the movie, but once they set aside their prejudices and saw each other correctly, it changed. Prejudice is from two words put together - pre and judge. As believers we should not pre-judge. In the movie, Gerry has a car accident and is in the hospital. Julius is the only one he wants to see. When Julius comes to the room Gerry asks the nurse, who says that only kin is allowed, if she is blind and wants to know why she cannot see the family resemblance because Julius is his brother. Then he tells Julius that he was afraid of him, and he only saw what he was afraid of, but now he realizes that he was only hating his brother. At the end of the movie, Sheryl Yost, is narrating at Gerry's funeral and says that people say that black and white can't work, but here we make it work every day. We have our disagreements, of course, but before we reach for hate always, always, we remember the Titans. (11). This movie demonstrates the beauty of love, humility and how we should lead with love and walk in truth, empowered by the Holy Spirit.

CHAPTER NINE

Wealth and Poverty: The Balance of Finances

Wealth and poverty. Is it really about the money? Most of us think so. When I was growing up, we were poor. My mother had at least a dozen sayings about being poor, most likely because that is how she grew up as well. One that comes to mind is: 'I don't have two nickels to rub together.' Not sure what that meant because when I had two nickels, I never rubbed them together. 'Waiting for my ship to come in," was another of those sayings. That one made sense after I became older and understood the shipping business. Growing up poor and not having very much money at all, we had to be self-sufficient. We had a dairy farm, and so we had cows, chickens, and a variety of farm animals. We also had three gardens, fruit trees, and berry bushes. We canned what we didn't eat fresh to help us through the winter. Needless to say, it was a lot of work.

When I left the farm to go to college I never really looked back. I did not miss all the work or the three gardens! One of my college roommates became like a brother to me, and I was also close with his family. His mom wanted to grow lots of things, but his dad wanted no part of a garden. Maybe he also had three gardens as a boy. He told me something that made sense. He said that he could work a couple of hours of overtime and have enough money to buy everything they needed without all the work of a garden. I liked that mentality, and I had a good job then as a single guy, so I incorporated that thinking into my mindset about having a farm or a garden. Why is all this important? Because growing up the way I did gave me a poverty mindset about money. Because we never had enough, I was convinced that I would never have enough as well. A poverty mindset is not a Scriptural mindset. Why? Because a Scriptural mindset knows God and trusts Him to provide everything. Trusting God is not easy, especially when we are immature believers, but it is what is best for us. When we look at the Scripture there is much about the subject of money, here is a breakdown:

> *The Bible contains roughly five hundred verses on prayer and faith, but well over two thousand verses on money, and approximately 40% of Jesus's parables deal with money—it's obvious that God has plenty to say about wealth and giving. (13) What would possibly be the reason that there is so much in the Bible about money? Jesus tells us exactly why: 24 "No one can serve two masters; for either he will hate the one and love the other, or he will be devoted to one*

and despise the other. You cannot serve God and wealth. Matthew 6:21. Paul adds: 6 But godliness actually is a means of great gain when accompanied by contentment. 7 For we have brought nothing into the world, so we cannot take anything out of it either. 8 If we have food and covering, with these we shall be content. 9 But those who want to get rich fall into temptation and a snare and many foolish and harmful desires which plunge men into ruin and destruction. 10 For the love of money is a root of all sorts of evil, and some by longing for it have wandered away from the faith and pierced themselves with many griefs. 11 But flee from these things, you man of God... 1 Timothy 6:6-11a. Does all this mean that God wants us to be poor? If not, there sure are a lot of poor people in the world. Actually, it is not about being poor, it is about being consumed by the love and gathering of money. Here is a statistic about per capita income yearly in 2018, The average per capita income worldwide is $10,298, according to the World Bank — and the differences in income between the poorest countries and richest countries in the world is staggering. Per capita annual incomes worldwide range from $280 in Burundi to $82,230 in Norway, with the U.S. in between *at $56,180. (14)*

These statistics show us that there are many poor people in the world. These people may struggle with having enough money, but they do not struggle with the love of money and all the evils that come with it. Trying to find a balance in the Kingdom between wealth and poverty is a struggle but not just for people who are directly in ministry and depend on donations to live, such as local church pastors. Most of the out of balance that is in the church today is not in the pulpit but in the pew.

There is much in the media today about preachers who bilk people out of their money. This seems to be a problem that has been going on for many years. These health and wealth preachers may be in the ministry for the wrong reason, but whatever their situation God is their judge. The same is true for the people in the pew, but those people never make the news. Here is a pertinent question, does the average church goer who sits in the pew tithe? If the average family in the US makes $50,000 a year and there are thirty families in the church, shouldn't the budget be $5,000 times thirty or $180,000 a year? And that is just the tithe, what about offerings? The church is out of balance in the area of money for sure. Years ago, when a mega church pastor was reporting his salary there was a question about him making over $70,000 while pastoring a church of over ten thousand members.

At the same time, a Fortune 500 company was paying

district managers over $200,000. The districts at that time had approximately five thousand employees for which the manager was responsible. So, half the responsibility and more than double the pay. If that manager were talking to the average person on the street the majority would have been congratulatory about his pay. We should wonder if the sentiment would have been the same for a pastor of over ten thousand making $70,000. I worked in the corporate world and as a supervisor of twenty to twenty-five people I was paid over $80,000. No one ever told me I was making too much money. The question for those that make a top living is where is your heart when it comes to money?

Here is where it gets sticky in the minds and hearts of believers. Do we really trust God in the area of finances and with 'our' money? Then what difference does it make if we can trust other people? The question is: Can we trust God? Do we trust God, and how much do we trust God with money. Imagine that you don't trust your church leadership with money. What do you do with your tithes and offerings? Do you give them to another church or ministry? Do you get to keep 'your' money because others cannot be trusted with it? I'm sure that we all wished it worked that way with our taxes. But seriously, what would you do? Go to another church? Can anyone be trusted with money? Can we? Do we trust God to do what He wants with 'our' money? This is where the real balance is in finances. We must balance discernment with trust. Unfortunately, we come down on the side of discernment because… after all its 'our' money.

Then we come up with all kinds of clever dodges to hold onto more of our money. If we believe in tithe and give ten percent, what ten percent do you give? Is it ten percent on the net or on the gross? Proverbs 3:10, AMPC, says: *Honor the Lord with your capital and sufficiency [from righteous labors] and with the first fruits of all your income;* There are many more Scriptures verses about first fruits and tithes. This is a good study if you have questions about how God sees the blessing that He gives us whether that's money or something else. In Genesis 28:20-22 we read: *20 Then Jacob made a vow, saying, "If God will be with me and will keep me on this journey that I take, and will give me food to eat and garments to wear, 21 and I return to my father's house in safety, then the Lord will be my God. 22 This stone, which I have set up as a pillar, will be God's house, and of all that You give me I **will surely give a tenth to You.***"

When we think about tithe and a percentage, do we see that economy of the Kingdom of Heaven differently than the economy of the country in which we live? If we live in the US, our federal tax is taken from our gross pay at whatever the federal percentage is currently. If it is 20% and we make 100 dollars, then we pay 20 dollars. The state tax is paid by us also. Now we are down to 80 dollars after our federal tax is taken, since the state government is a lesser authority, they should take from the 80, but they do not. They take from the gross of $100. If they take 5% then the tax is 5 dollars. Now we are down to $75. Then all the other government entries that take from our direct pay do the same thing until our net pay is around 69 dollars. Most people then tithe on the net pay of 69 dollars. But does this 'tithe' honor God? In the following passage the priests are held accountable, but who is bringing the bad offerings? Not the priests! This is a long passage, but the content is very pertinent. Malachi 1:6-14: *"'A son honors his father, and a servant his master. Then if I am a father, where is My honor? And if I am a master, where is My respect? Says the Lord of hosts to you, O priests who despise My name. But you say, 'How have we despised Your name?' 7 You are presenting defiled food upon My altar. But you say, 'How have we defiled You?' In that you say, 'The table of the Lord is to be despised.' 8 But when you present the blind for sacrifice, is it not evil? And when you present the lame and sick, is it not evil? Why not offer it to your governor? Would he be pleased with you? Or would he receive you kindly?" says the Lord of hosts. 9 "But now will you not entreat God's favor, that He may be gracious to us? With such an offering on your part, will He receive any of you kindly?" says the Lord of hosts. 10 "Oh that there were one among you who would shut the gates, that you might not uselessly kindle fire on My altar! I am not pleased with you," says the Lord of hosts, "nor will I accept an offering from you. 11 For from the rising of the sun even to its setting, My name will be great among the nations, and in every place incense is going to be offered to My name, and a grain offering that is pure; for My name will be great among the nations," says the Lord of hosts. 12 "But you* *are profaning it, in that you say, 'The table of the Lord is defiled, and as for its fruit, its food is to be despised.' **13** You also say, 'My, how tiresome it is!' And you disdainfully sniff at it," says the Lord of hosts, "and you bring what was taken by robbery and what is lame or sick; so you bring the offering! Should I receive that from your hand?" says the Lord. **14** "But cursed be the swindler who has a male in his flock and vows it, but sacrifices a blemished animal to the Lord, for I am a great King," says the Lord of hosts, "and My name is feared among the nations."*

We read the Scripture but struggle to apply what God says to us. Now, since the sacrifices are completed in the death of Jesus, we no longer bring bulls and sheep. What we do bring should be a sacrifice that pleases God. The first thing we give is ourselves, (Romans 12:1-2) and then we ask the Lord what He wants from us. In the book of Acts the people who were saved brought everything and offered it up as a sacrifice. Acts 4:32-35, reads: *32 And the congregation of those who believed were of one heart and soul; and not one of them claimed that anything belonging to him was his own, but all things were common property to them. 33 And with great power the apostles were giving testimony to the resurrection of the Lord Jesus, and abundant grace was upon them all. 34 For there was not a needy person among them, for all who were owners of land or houses would sell them and bring the proceeds of the sales 35 and lay them at the apostles feet, and they would be distributed to each as any had need.*

The reality is that when we accept God, and the salvation that He has provided, He does not want part of us, but He wants all of us; everything.

Years ago, we were at a Sunday morning service in a different state and a church we had never attended. There was a special speaker that day, and he picked my wife and me out of the crowd to minister to us. At the end of the service the pastor of the church stood to take an offering for this speaker and his family who were missionaries abroad. When the offering started, I prayed and asked the Lord how much He wanted me to give in the offering. My answer came as a question when I heard in my spirit the question: *How much did I give for you?* The obvious answer was - everything! So, I gave all the money that I had on me at that moment. If you are struggling with this part of the book and how much you should give to God, then how about starting at ten percent. And if you want to call it a first fruit offering then God should get first place. Set aside the ten percent of the gross and give that to the Lord.

Some people say that the tithe is not in the New Testament, that the writers of the New Testament do not talk about a tithe, or ten percent, and that tithing is an Old Testament concept. This is true, and we see the tithe long before the law in the book of Exodus. Is the reason that it is not clearly stated in the New Testament because there was no need for correction, and the tithe was not an issue then? Maybe. But giving to God has been something that believers have been compelled to do all the way back to

Genesis 4. What we need to understand is that wherever we stand on this issue we need to stand there with a clear conscious before our Lord and Savior.

What is the balance between poverty and wealth? God promises an abundant life, but we struggle with what that means. Peace with God is certainly essential to having abundance. Stress and anxiety rob us of peace, and we find ourselves struggling to feel any abundance in our lives. Philippians 4:6-7 says: *Be anxious for nothing, but in everything by prayer and supplication with thanksgiving let your requests be made known to God. 7 And the peace of God, which surpasses all comprehension, will guard your hearts and your minds in Christ Jesus.*

We can seek God, and ask for His clarity on anything that we are struggling with in this life. James 1:5 reads: *5 But if any of you lacks wisdom, let him ask of God, who gives to all generously and without reproach, and it will be given to him.* Trusting God with everything, being at peace, and having gratitude can certainly help us feel that our lives are more abundant. The balance is seeking God and following what it is that He wants us to do in every situation.

CHAPTER TEN

Spirit, Soul and Flesh: The Balance of Living

This is an area of teaching that is much needed and one where there really is not a 'divine tension' until salvation.

Paul talks about the tension, or struggle, to find balance between the spirit and the flesh in Romans chapter seven. However we choose to look at that passage and others in the Scriptures, we need to realize that the tension is not what brings balance, but rather, the tension is what demonstrates us being out of balance. What we need to see is that there is a balance across all three of these parts of humanity: body, soul and spirit, but that balance is found in the spirit rule of the flesh and the mind, or soul. Spirit rule is a cooperative endeavor. It is our spirit submitting to the Holy Spirit. For this chapter, to alleviate any confusion, I will use the word spirit when referencing the spirit of humanity. Then I will use the words Holy Spirit to reference the Spirit of the Lord.

The duality of spirit, our spirit, and the Holy Spirit, is important to understand because Ephesians says that we were dead before salvation. Most theologians believe that the spirit is what was dead. I agree, but maybe not the way that most theologians would expect. My understanding of this subject comes from the teaching Jesus gave to Nicodemus about being born again in John 3. John's gospel also first mentions being born again in chapter one. We also know that the Word of God is seed in the parable of the farmer from Matthew's gospel chapter thirteen about the wheat and the tares. Matthew thirteen also has the story of the parable of the Sower. The seed is sown into the hearts of humans. One of the Greek words for seed is: πέρμα *spérma, sper'-mah; from G4687; something sown, i.e. seed (including the male "sperm"); by implication, offspring; specially, a remnant (figuratively, as if kept over for planting):—issue, seed.* This Greek word *spérma,* is from, or based on, another Greek word: σπείρω, *speírō, spi'-ro; probably strengthened from G4685 (through the idea of extending); to scatter, i.e. sow (literally or figuratively):— sow(- er), receive seed.*

The Parable of the Wheat and Tares uses the root Greek word speiro, and the parable of the wheat and tares uses the Greek word sperma. Obviously, this word in Strong's as number G4690 is the Greek from which we get our English word sperm. The male half of what is needed to conceive a human baby. John gives us more information to put together with the Gospel of John chapters 1 and 3 in 1 John 3:9: *Whosoever is born of God does not commit sin; for his seed remains in him: and he cannot sin, because he is born of God.* This word seed is the Greek word sperma. We are born again by the seed of the Word of God sown in our hearts. There is a conception that takes place in us, and the 'deadness' of the spirit in us is born of the seed of the Holy Spirit. This creates the duality of spirit and Spirit within us. It is like the two natures in Jesus of divine and human. Though it is obviously not the same as Jesus since he was born of a virgin birth. But it is important to understand and gives context to what Paul was talking about in the tension between the flesh and the spirit in Romans 7.

What we are going to look at now is an understanding of the balance of the three parts of humanity. Being out of balance causes tension, and that results in many problems for us humans. The balance is found in spirit rule, or as Paul calls it, walking in the Holy Spirit. What we need to grasp is the concept of integration and our part in that integration of body, soul, and spirit. Therefore, the purpose of this next teaching is to give us a deeper understanding of integration. The definition of integrate is: *to form, coordinate, or blend into a functioning or unified whole.* The best way to understand integration is to better understand each part of the three-part balance. This flows out of an understanding of the three-part makeup of humanity. We are body, soul, and spirit. Interestingly, Paul lists these the opposite of how we list them. The Hebrew listing puts the most important first, and we tend to 'save the best for last.' Paul lists them this way: *23 Now may the God of peace Himself sanctify you entirely; and may your spirit and soul and body be preserved complete, without blame at the coming of our*

Lord Jesus Christ. 1 Thessalonians 5:23.

Therefore, we as humans, are body, soul and spirit. The body is made up of flesh, blood, and bones and gives us world consciousness through the five senses of smell, sight, touch, taste, and hearing. We know and experience the world around us through these five body senses. The soul gives us self-consciousness, and is comprised of mind, will, and emotions. We know ourselves better than any other human knows us, we are self-aware of who we are as a person. The spirit is made up of wisdom, communion, and conscience. The spirit gives us God consciousness and the three parts of spirit are energized by the Holy Spirit. Jesus tells us that: *24 God is [a]spirit, and those who worship Him must worship in spirit and truth."* John 4:24. The only way to connect and have communion with God is through spirit and truth. We must come to God in spirit not in flesh or soul, and we have to come in truth. Lies cannot be in the presence of God the Father. Of course, there are many things that cannot be in the presence of God including our flesh. This is why no one can look upon the face of God and live, no one in the flesh. In the spirit we can look upon the face of God. (Isaiah 6 and Revelation 4)

SOUL

Mind is a description of the mental part of who we are as humans. This part is more than just what we think, reason, or rationalize. It is also our emotional part and our will. We can, therefore, understand that the mind or soul is made up of mind, will, and emotion. We may call the mind our consciousness. Let's look at them as parts of the whole of our soul.

RATIONAL

What is the rational part of the mind? We need to define it here so there is no confusion about the other parts of mind. The rational part of the soul or our mind is the thinking or reasoning part. The rational, logical, analytical aspect of the mind is the part of the mind that gives us decision making capability. In decision making the rational part of mind weighs things and makes conclusions before decisions are made. We also need to know that the emotional part of mind may override the rational and make a hastily decision based on an emotional response that could have drastic consequences. As an example, people within the strong emotion of rage tend to make unwise choices that can have devastating consequences.

EMOTION

Our emotions are feeling responses to external and internal stimuli. These responses fall into positive and negative categories. There are positive responses to external stimuli, and there are positive responses to internal stimuli. Some of the external stimuli that provoke a positive response are love, compassion, and kindness demonstrated toward us by others. Then there are internal stimuli that provoke a positive response such as good memories and meditation or prayer.

There are negative responses to external stimuli and negative responses to internal stimuli. The negative responses may be the result of trauma we have experienced. These traumas may be mental, emotional, and physical in nature. All types of traumas are linked to our emotions both in what has happened to us and our response to what has happened to us. Negative responses are responses that can also be the result of emotional trauma.

There are external stimuli that provoke a negative response. These may be things such as historical events like human bondage or the Holocaust. Things that have happened in the past that invoke an emotional response. There may also be current events, things that are happening in the present that invoke an emotional response such as a terrorist attack or a shooting in our town or region or a death in our family. These negative events may be things that happen directly to us such as physical harm where the body is hurt such as falling, physical abuse or sexual abuse. They may also be emotional trauma where our feelings are hurt such as verbal abuse, neglect, or abandonment.

There are internal negative things as well, these are internal stimuli that provoke a negative response such as self-talk or thinking and speaking negatively about oneself. There is regret and bitterness which are all internal stimuli that provoke a negative response in us.

WILL

Once we decide (reason, rationalize, consider choices) then we will, move, or respond to bring that decision to pass. We can think about what we want for breakfast and even reach a decision to go out to eat, but if we never get off the couch then breakfast never happens. If we have to move or act upon the decision we have made in order to accomplish it, this then becomes an act of our will. There are many struggles with our will, and we often want to change them with what we call New Year's resolutions. These resolutions don't often last for very long because as Jesus said, the spirit is willing, but the flesh is weak. Though there are many and varied issues here, only some of the will struggles will be identified. Addictions are a serious will struggle. Addictions are anything to which we have given power that overcomes our will such as, drugs, sex, food, alcohol, work, or physical activity. Codependency is another issue we can struggle with in our will. Codependency is when we lose ourselves in a relationship with someone, and our will becomes dominated by another. Oxford defines it as *excessive emotional or psychological reliance on a partner, typically one who requires support on account of an illness or addiction.*

BODY

What is body? It is that part of us that is physical and material in nature. The body is composed of flesh, blood, and bones. It is that part of us that senses physicality. This is communicated to the mind or soul and spirit through the five senses of touch, smell, hearing, sight, and taste. The body is the vehicle through which we interact in the physical world. Paul rightly calls it the house in which we live. The 'earthen vessel' that allows us to physically interact with the physical world. When people die and the physical body is no longer able to sustain or house the soul and spirit then they move out into an incorporeal state. We are no longer able to interact in the physical realm. Our voice, speech and movement all become incomprehensible to everything that remains in the physical realm. This is part of the reason why the enemy and his minions desire possession. This gives them access to the physical realm.

Though there is some power that they possess in the physical realm it is not the same as having possession of a physical body. We can think of it as an illustration of being in a virtual world. We create virtual avatars that can interact in a virtual world while we sit in our chairs and hold the controller. Or we might think of it like the movie, *The Matrix*. The enemy desires to be in the matrix, but he needs a physical body to do so. On the flip side, we are in the physical realm, and we often don't think that the spirit realm is more constant and real than the physical realm. The spirit realm is more real than the physical realm because it is unchanging. God is the only Being who does not need a physical body to operate in the physical world we live in. This is true because He is the Creator of this physical universe.

Thinking about our physical bodies, the body can experience trauma which, if left unchecked, can cause serious and deadly harm. The body also experiences a wide variety of diseases and physical ailments. When these types of physical trauma and ailments are not corrected, they can have an impact on the mind. Physical pain can be like a dagger in the mind blocking all else. We can learn to endure physical pain, but it always takes a toll on us.

DEATH

Death comes to us all because eventually the body deteriorates to the point where there is a separation of the mind, (soul) and spirit from the body. The real, unchanging part of us enters the spirit realm, and we are separated from the physical realm. Interestingly, the soul or mind, our consciousness, can in fact grow and change. But what it is made of cannot. So, in one sense our soul can change and in another it is unchangeable. Spirit can be in the physical realm, but flesh cannot be in the spirit realm.

The word death in the New Testament is the Greek word θάνατος, transliterated to: thánatos, pronounced: than'-at-os. One of the meanings is: 'that separation (whether natural or violent) of the soul and the body by which the life on earth is ended.' (12)

SPIRIT

What is the spirit? Spirit is that part of man that can connect to divine. Spirit is energized by divine. (Life giving). Spirit gains wisdom by connection to divine. Spirit is enlightened by connection to divine. (conscience). Spirit is inspired by connection to divine. (communion) We must become spirit connected for all of these to take place. It is not something that most adults do naturally. Children are more naturally open in their spirits and can be born again more easily than adults. Children have a keen sense in the spirit realm that is hobbled when they become adults. This sense opens them up to the spirit realm, and they accept it more naturally than adults accept the spirit realm. As a way that God communicates with us, and especially children. Years ago, a band called Supertramp put words to this sense and those words give us a verbal way to understand something that is nonverbal. Please look up the lyrics to a Supertramp song called the "Logical Song," and read there what I am trying to express here.

CONNECTING TO SPIRIT

This connecting is our spirit to the Holy Spirit - the Spirit of the Creator. When we become born again there is life in the spirit that gives us the connection to the Holy

Spirit. What we must learn to do is discern the difference between what is soul, or mind, and what is spirit. We begin a journey at spirit conception that is about teaching us to trust God, connect to God, and learning to walk in the Spirit with God. The primary thing that we need to learn is to hear the voice of God more clearly when there are so many voices clamoring for our attention. Jesus said: *14 I am the good shepherd, and I know My own and My own know Me, 15 even as the Father knows Me and I know the Father; and I lay down My life for the sheep. 16 I have other sheep, which are not of this fold; I must bring them also, and they will hear My voice; and they will become one flock with one shepherd. 27 My sheep hear My voice, and I know them, and they follow Me; 28 and I give eternal life to them, and they will never perish; and no one will snatch them out of My hand.* John 10:14-16, 27-18.

It can become easy to discern the voice of the Lord in the midst of everything going on around us in this world. One of the primary ways to hear the Lord is in the pages of Scripture. There is a reason why the Bible is the most loved book in some circles and the most hated in other circles. It is impossible to read the Scripture with an open heart and mind and not be changed by it. That is why there is so much Scripture in this book. It is the foundation that we must stand on as believers, and it fosters the spirit to Holy Spirit connection that is necessary to walk in the Spirit.

WISDOM

Wisdom from God begins with the fear of God and the Scripture. The reason for this truth is that we must learn about God and have a relationship with Him. We can know that God exists as we study the natural world around us, but to know God, He must reveal Himself in a more personal and knowable way. Special revelation is needed for us to understand God and His ways. This is where we find God revealed in the Scriptures. The Scriptures say: *the fear of the Lord is the beginning of wisdom; all who follow his precepts have good understanding.* Psalms 110:10. *The fear of the Lord is the beginning of knowledge, but fools despise wisdom and instruction,* Proverbs 1:7. The word 'fear' is not to be afraid of God or the fear of dread or punishment. This fear is the fear of awe or reverence. God is to be feared when we think about Who He is and who we are in His presence. Paul calls this the terror of the Lord in 2 Corinthians 5:11. This awe of God is where true wisdom begins. Why is the fear of the Lord the beginning of wisdom? Because those who know God fear Him. They have a reverential awe and respect for God that only comes out of truly knowing Him.

Why are some people not afraid to say what they say and do what they do? Paul gives us a list in Romans 3 of issues with people who have no understanding about God. He ends it with the culmination in verse 18: *"There is no fear of God before their eyes."* Paul is quoting Psalms 36:1.

Read that psalm for some more understanding. When we think of wisdom these are some of the things that we must keep in mind. The Scriptures tell us that there are two kinds of wisdom. Worldly, earthly, or sensual wisdom and the wisdom that is from above. The way to see this is to think about some hero with superpowers like Superman and his strength. Humans have strength, but Superman has super strength. Man has wisdom or logic, but God has super wisdom and super logic. Paul tells us this in 1 Corinthians 2:3-17: *3 I was with you in weakness and in fear and in much trembling, 4 and my message and my preaching were not in persuasive words of wisdom, but in demonstration of the Spirit and of power, 5 so that your faith would not rest on the wisdom of men, but on the power of God. 6 Yet we do speak **wisdom** among those who are mature; a **wisdom**, however, not of this age nor of the rulers of this age, who are passing away; 7 but we speak **God's wisdom** in a mystery, the **hidden wisdom** which God predestined before the ages to our glory; 8 **the wisdom** which none of the rulers of this age has understood; for if they had understood it (**wisdom**) they would not have crucified the Lord of glory;* Powerful words describing the difference that James talks about in chapter three of his letter. *13 Who is wise and understanding among you? Let him show by good conduct that his works are done in the meekness of wisdom. 14 But if you have bitter envy and self-seeking in your hearts, do not boast and lie against the truth. 15 This wisdom does not descend from above, but is earthly, sensual, demonic. 16 For where envy and self-seeking exist, confusion and every evil thing* *are there. 17 But the wisdom that is from above is first pure, then peaceable, gentle, willing to yield, full of mercy and good fruits, without partiality and without hypocrisy.*

Supernatural wisdom, that's what God gives, and James mentions it his letter chapter one: *2 My brethren, count it all joy when you fall into various trials, 3 knowing that the testing of your faith produces patience. 4 But let patience have its perfect work, that you may be perfect and complete, lacking nothing. 5 If any of you lacks **wisdom**, let him ask of God, who gives (**wisdom**) to all liberally and without reproach, and it (**wisdom**) will be given to him. 6 But let him ask in faith, with no doubting,* This is why true wisdom is part of our spirit. True wisdom resonates in the spirit of those who are born again. And it seems foolish to others, *18 For the message of the cross is foolishness to those who are perishing, but to us who are being saved it is the power of God. 19 For it is written: "I will destroy the **wisdom** of the **wise** And bring to nothing the understanding of the prudent." 20 Where is the **wise**? Where is the scribe? Where is the disputer of this age? Has not God made foolish the **wisdom** of this world? 21 For since, in the **wisdom** of God, the world through **wisdom** did not know God, it pleased God through the foolishness of the message preached to save those who believe. 22 For Jews request a sign, and Greeks seek after **wisdom**; 23 but we preach Christ crucified, to the Jews a stumbling block and to the Greeks foolishness, 24 but to those who are called, both Jews and Greeks, Christ the power of God and the*

wisdom *of God. 25 Because the foolishness of God is* **wiser** *than men, and the weakness of God is stronger than men.* 1 Corinthians 1:18-25.

Again, powerful words about the two types of wisdom. Which should we seek as believers in the One True God? The answer is clear, and we have not even looked at the encouragement to seek wisdom found in the book of Proverbs. You can read that encouragement in Proverbs for yourself armed with an understanding about the two kinds of wisdom and which one is better.

COMMUNION

What is communion? We have all heard the answer that it is a union of the things we have in common, or a common union. When we think about what communion is in the Holy Spirit it is much more than a union of what we have in common. This is because we do not have much in common with God. He is wholly different from us. Communion between human and divine is more of a receiving of what we need from the source of everything. This makes the most sense as we understand and believe that God is the beginning, middle, and end of everything. *33 Oh, the depth of the riches both of the wisdom and knowledge of God! How unsearchable are His judgments and unfathomable His ways! 34 For who has known the mind of the Lord, or who became His counselor? 35 Or who has first given to Him that it might be paid back to him again? 36 For from*

Him and through Him and to Him are all things. To Him be the glory forever. Amen. Romans 11:33-36.

Read that passage again slowly, and consider all that Paul says about God in those few verses. My pastor once preached a whole series of messages on just verse 36, teaching us the depth of who God is and how connected He is to everything. When we neglect this connection for communion or cut it off altogether, we sever and alienate ourselves from the source of all life. God does everything He does for us, not for Him. He has need of nothing. We, however, need God for our next breath. Theologians call what God does for His creation, every moment, common grace. *15 He (Jesus) is the image of the invisible God, the firstborn of all creation. 16 For by Him all things were created, both in the heavens and on earth, visible and invisible, whether thrones or dominions or rulers or authorities—all things have been created through Him and for Him. 17 He is before all things, and **in Him all things hold together**.* Colossians 3:15-17 Everything is held together by God. All the way down to the atoms which were mentioned in the introduction to what scientists call the strong nuclear attraction. The very atoms that make up the air we breathe are held together by God. If He removed Himself from His creation it would cease to exist.

Here is why communion with God is so important. We receive from Him everything we need to live a life that aligns with Him. Without Him there is only decay and death. So, communion with God is spirit to Holy Spirit. This is the only way to connect to God. Without the Holy Spirit, and truth, there is no connection to God. *23 But an hour is coming, and now is, when the true worshipers will worship the Father in spirit and truth; for such people the Father seeks to be His worshipers. 24 God is spirit, and those who worship Him must worship in spirit and truth."* John 4:23-24 Worship is a way to connect and commune with God. Jesus tells us here that we must connect to God in spirit - our spirit to His Holy Spirit. Years ago, this was called mysticism. Now, since there has been an exposure to more eastern religions, like Hinduism, and their understanding of mystic connection, a lot of fundamental evangelical Christians see mystic connections as abhorrent. We should be careful to remain Scriptural without aligning ourselves with darkness. Often, if we dig deeply into the history of some of the things that we see as wrong or off, we find that there is a spiritual or Scriptural foundation.

A current illustration is the rainbow. There has been a change in the representation of the rainbow, and now it's not something that believers want to associate with because of the change. What we need to do as believers is understand what is Scriptural and what is not, and stand on those things without being afraid of the truth. Augustine once said, 'The truth is like a lion, we don't have to defend it. Let is loose; it will defend itself.' Holy Spirit to our spirit is a Scriptural principle that matters as we seek wisdom, truth, and direction from God.

CONSCIENCE

Conscience is that part of us that warns us when we are about to do something wrong and convicts us when we have done something wrong. In the age of grace, since the death and resurrection of Jesus, the Holy Spirt has been sent. Part of the Holy Spirit's role is described by Jesus in John 16:7-11: *7 But I tell you the truth, it is to your advantage that I go away; for if I do not go away, the Helper will not come to you; but if I go, I will send Him to you. 8 And He,* ***when He comes, will convict the world concerning sin and righteousness and judgment****; 9 concerning sin, because they do not believe in Me; 10 and concerning righteousness, because I go to the Father and you no longer see Me; 11 and concerning judgment, because the ruler of this world has been judged.*

The Holy Spirit is the voice of truth to all humanity of what is right and what is wrong. There is not a clear indication of the role of the Holy Spirit before Pentecost, but it is plain what part of His role is since then from the word Jesus gave to the disciples. Seems to me that it is hard to ignore the prompting of the Holy Spirit. In 1 Timothy 4, Paul talks about some departing from the faith and then searing their conscience with a hot iron. We may not understand fully what Paul was saying, but the implication is that these people 'fell from faith' and they began to listen to the voices of darkness. Giving in to those things that are not Scriptural, or Holy in any way, sears the conscience.

There was a believing man who was married and started a relationship with a married woman. This man had five children and the woman had two. The relationship turned sexual, which is adultery based on the Scriptures, and even the secular court systems. They eventually got divorced and now live together. The man then told someone that, "I am alright with Jesus," This is an example of listening to the voices of darkness and then having your conscience seared to the point that sin is no longer sin even if two families and many lives are devastated in the wake of this sin. Believers have their activated conscience energized by the Holy Spirt as the final part of the spirit of humanity. The activated Holy Spirit conscience begins to convict the believer of things that were normal to them before.

I remember thinking before I got saved that taking the Lord's name in vain by saying, "Jesus" when I was mad was the least of the swear words, and the worst was saying the 'f' word. After I was saved, saying "Jesus" when I was mad and not using His name properly became the worst of the swear words. If we allow the Holy Spirit to energize our activated conscience it can become part of our guidance for walking in right relationship with God. Was the writer of Hebrews talking about a highly activated and sensitive conscience when he wrote: *12...you have come to need milk and not solid food. 13 For everyone who partakes only of milk is not accustomed to the word of righteousness, for he is an infant. 14 But solid food is for the mature, **who because of practice have their senses trained to discern***

good and evil. We can train our conscience under the tutelage of the Holy Spirit to be sensitive to good and evil. Being good or holy is like the truth, we do not have to defend what is good, we just must live holy and that will be enough.

INTEGRATION OF SPIRIT, SOUL, AND BODY. BRINGING BALANCE TO OUR WHOLE BEING.

The last part of this chapter is about finding, striking, or however you may choose to say it, a balance in the whole of our being. We must be careful not to neglect one aspect of our being over another or focus our attention on one part and forget that there are other parts to our being whole. The best way to do this is to understand each part or aspect. Hopefully, the previous part of the chapter has given us what we need. Once we understand each part it becomes easier to integrate all three into one unified whole being. If we lived as a unified whole being, then we are living as we were created to live. We are living in balance, and we understand what it means to be fully human. It is helpful to understand integration. When we think about integration it is the completion of the definition of the word integration, which is: *to form, coordinate, or blend into a functioning or unified whole.* So how do we integrate spirit, soul, and body? This is best accomplished by determining that part of us that is out of balance and correcting it.

We may determine that there are many issues of all the three parts that are out of balance. So, then we determine which part is most out of balance and begin there.

MIND OUT OF BALANCE

The mind being out of balance results in many of the psychological/mental disorders that are described in psychology. Some are: Depression, Anxiety, Fear, Narcissism, DID, and many other mental disorders. Each one of the mental disorders is to be dealt with singularly and individually. However, there can be a positive benefit to group therapy. Group therapy usually is focused on an issue that everyone in the group has as a problem. A classic example is AA. Physical substance addictions are both mental and physical. A mind in balance is generally seen as a mind that is emotionally mature and at peace. Though there may sometimes be a shift up or down, baseline stability is more the norm.

BODY OUT OF BALANCE

The body being out of balance results in many of the physical ailments and/or diseases that occur in the body. Some things that cause body imbalance are eating habits, lack of physical activity, physical trauma, and/or disease of any kind. Often when we are out of balance physically it affects both soul and spirit. Jesus went about healing the bodies of people before He dealt with mental, emotional, or spiritual issues. Pain can be like a dagger in the mind consuming our thoughts and keeping us unable to focus on anything else. Physical wellness can often be the first step to mental and spiritual wellness.

SPIRIT OUT OF BALANCE

A spirit out of balance may result in both physical and mental issues. For example, bitterness can result in depression, anxiety and even arthritis. The spiritual exercise of forgiveness releases bitterness. If we refuse to forgive, Jesus has this to say in Matthew 6:14-15: *14 For if you forgive others for their transgressions, your heavenly Father will also forgive you. 15 But if you do not forgive others, then your Father will not forgive your transgressions.* Also, in Matthew 13:33-35, there is the parable of the kingdom about a wicked servant who was forgiven by the king but refused to forgive his fellow servant. The king summoned him and said: *33 Should you not also have had mercy on your fellow servant, in the same way that I had mercy on you? 34 And his lord, moved with anger, handed him over to the torturers until he should repay all that was owed him. 35 My heavenly Father will also do the same to you, if each of you does not forgive his brother from your heart.* Have you ever seen people obsessed with their anger, desire for vengeance, and bitterness toward another ...consumed by it? Would we not say that they are being tortured by their obsession? They keep it in the forefront of their mind and think about it all the time. They are totally focused on their pain and hurt and how to get the other person back. How to exact their pound of flesh until they feel the debt owed to them is paid in full. Forgiveness releases all that emotion. Forgiveness is about setting yourself free even before there is a setting free of the other person's debt. Forgiveness that is genuine, releases all the anger, bitterness, vengeance, and hate toward another. When we feel out of balance in the spirit, we should check our hearts and start with forgiveness. Sometimes, it is us needing to forgive and often it is us needing forgiveness. Firstly from God, because all sin is an offense toward Him, and then toward others in our lives.

Other examples of spirit being out of balance are no connection to the Holy Spirit, little or no understanding of the human spirit, and being ignorant of or ignoring the prompting of the Holy Spirit.

CHAPTER ELEVEN

Male and Female: The Divine Tension and Balance of Marriage

The Balance of the Sexes

UNDERSTANDING DESIGN

Hopefully, if you have gotten this far in the book, you realize that the perspective of the book is a Scriptural one. We may disagree about our positions on issues, but we should base what we believe on the teachings of Scripture.

Some may ask, are you really going to wade into this troubled water? The perspective here, as well, will be based on Scripture. We must realize that there are many ways to apply different Scriptures in various situations, but there should, or can truly be, only one interpretation. Too often, there are so many interpretations that we end up not agreeing on much when it comes to Scripture. This makes us study and study, examine, and read. Then, we need to filter what we read, or study, through the Holy Spirit, of whom Jesus said: *12 "I have much more to say to you, more than you can now bear. 13 But **when he, the Spirit of truth, comes, he will guide you into all the truth.** He will not speak on his own; he will speak only what he hears, and he will tell you what is yet to come. 14 He will glorify me because it is from me that he will receive what he will make known to you. 15 All that belongs to the Father is mine. That is why I said the Spirit will receive from me what he will make known to you."* When we do not filter all that, we read, study, or interpret through the Spirit we end up being like the 'lawyers' in the New Testament and like the Pharisee's.

We become self-absorbed through knowledge and pride and even when we are wrong, we think that we are right, and no one can tell us different because 'we know what the Scriptures say.' Jesus, in Matthew 22:29, told the Sadducees who were the ruling Priests in the Temple, along with the Sanhedrin, the 70 ruling elders: *29 Jesus answered and said unto them, You do err, not knowing the Scriptures, nor the power of God.*

We have modern day people who fit into this mindset, and often these are the people that are most trusted to interpret the Scriptures. We need the Word and the Spirit or 'power of God' to have balance. Having said all that, there will be much Scripture in this chapter, but you must allow the Holy Spirit of Truth to lead you into all truth.

This chapter will focus mainly on marriage and the

interaction between husband and wife, but there will be some references to singleness or the interaction of the sexes outside of marriage.

When God created Adam, we really do not have a lot of detail about the creation of Adam in the book of Genesis. The Scriptures seem to indicate that God created Adam fully grown, or at least that is the way that most people interpret what is written in Genesis. Is it possible that this assumption is wrong? We cannot say emphatically either way, but what we do know is that Jesus does not appear on the scene as a fully grown man, he comes as a baby and grows. He learns, matures, and grows in favor with God and men. Is it possible that God created Adam as a baby or child? We do know that God values maturity and the journey into maturity. How do we know? All things begin small and grow into maturity. We also do not know emphatically how Adam and Eve were together before God separated them in Genesis two. What is interesting, also, is that God called the first human He created, ADAM, which is not a name but more like a title. ADAM literally means humanity or mankind. Before there was toxic masculinity, people understood that the word man, in certain contexts, meant humanity. I agree with a more precise definition so there is no confusion. God created humanity in what we now understand as the being ADAM. Then after the naming of the animals God takes a side of Adam and fashions Eve. The old KJV does not give a clear meaning when it says 'rib.' Actual ribs are on our sides, but they are also on our fronts and backs, hence the term rib cage. The word for side is the Hebrew word and Strongs Dictionary H6763, עֵלָע tsêlâ', tsay-law.' The KJV translates Strong's H6763 in the following manner: side (19x), chamber (11x), boards (2x), corners (2x), rib (2x), another (1x), beams (1x), halting (1x), leaves (1x), planks (1x). (16).

Then God took one of Adam's sides to fashion Eve. This makes better sense when we think of ADAM as humanity rather than as a man in modern terms. God took a side of ADAM and fashioned Eve. What side He took is not revealed. That side may have been more than most Bible readers believe or can understand. In some of the Jewish traditional writings we read this, *"And the L-rd G-d caused a deep sleep to fall upon man, and he slept, and He took one of his sides, and He closed the flesh in its place. And the L-rd G-d built the side that He had taken from man into a woman..."* (Genesis: 2:21-2) In the first chapter of Genesis we are told, *"G-d created man in his image, in the image of G-d He created him, male and female He created them"* (Genesis 1:27). According to the Midrash, Talmud and Zohar, the original human, Adam, was first created as a "double faced" being, made up of a male and female joined at the back. Fused together the figures in the painting reflect man as a two-sided creature with one face male, and one face female. After this primordial uncoupling, an everlasting yearning to reconnect remains between every man and woman as well as the hope that they can now meet each other face to face, a level of intimacy greater than unity." (17).

Rabbi Samual ben Nahman was of the late 3rd century. Nahman's suggestion has an exegetical basis: The passage in Genesis begins by referring to Adam in the singular, but then says that God created "them" male and female. Was it one being or two? Nahman answers by saying that it was one being that had both genders. Resh Lakish is from a slightly earlier date, born 200 AD. Lakish's suggestion also has an exegetical basis. If Genesis 1 records the creation of males and females, how is it that Adam in Genesis 2, which immediately follows, has no partner? Lakish answers that Adam did have a partner on his back, but that this was not the ideal way of creating a male-female couple, and so God divided them into two people. (18).

God has created some very interesting beings that are part of the creation. Read this description in Ezekiel 1:5-11: *5 Within it there were figures resembling four living beings. And this was their appearance: they had human form. 6 Each of them had four faces and four wings. 7 Their legs were straight, and their feet were like a calf's hoof, and they gleamed like burnished bronze. 8 Under their wings on their four sides were human hands. As for the faces and wings of the four of them, 9 their wings touched one another; their faces did not turn when they moved, each went straight forward. 10 As for the form of their faces, each had the face of a man; all four had the face of a lion on the right and the face of a bull on the left, and all four had the face of an eagle. 11 Such were their faces.*

Their wings were spread out above; each had two touching another being, and two covering their bodies.

These ancient writings constitute some interesting points about the creation of ADAM and the separation of Eve. As always, you must make up your own minds based on Scripture and the leading of the Holy Spirit. We are prone to choose one way or the other but to not consider both. Firstly, we base only what we believe in Scripture and do not listen to the Holy Spirit's leading. This usually results in misinterpretation of the Scripture. Secondly, we believe that we are being led by the Holy Spirit apart from Scripture or often in defiance of Scripture. Usually, the spirit behind this type of behavior is not the Holy Spirit. Therefore, this behavior is rebellion.

This understanding of the creation of ADAM gives clarity to why there is to be harmony in the marriage relationship. Intimacy is to be face to face, and the joining of the bodies creates a oneness that God intended for marriage and family. Physiologically, when there is intimacy and pleasure in the sexual union, the hormone oxytocin is released which has been called the 'love hormone.' Researchers believe that oxytocin's influence on reward pathways creates a positive behavior loop for engaging in social and sexual contact with a reliable, monogamous partner.' (19).

This affect is the binding of the oneness of a couple. Illicit sexual unions create a soul tie to the person with whom you have sexual contact. This is the negative result of sinful behavior which is the opposite of the pure behavior of a married couple. This is why Paul wrote in 1 Corinthians 6: *15 Do you not know that your bodies are members of Christ? Shall I then take away the members of Christ and make them members of a prostitute? May it never be! 16 Or do you not know that the one who joins himself to a prostitute is one body with her? For He says, "The two shall become one flesh." 17 But the one who joins himself to the Lord is one spirit with Him. 18 Flee immorality. Every other sin that a man commits is outside the body, but the immoral man sins against his own body. 19 Or do you not know that your body is a temple of the Holy Spirit who is in you, whom you have from God, and that you are not your own? 20 For you have been bought with a price: therefore, glorify God in your body.*

The sexual union was designed by God. There are many purposes infused in the proper sexual intimacy of a husband and wife. When we stray from this God given design, we invite all kinds of darkness into our lives. We need to see these designs of God as guardrails created for us to enjoy what God has designed. They are not fences to keep us from something fun or exciting. Therefore, we realize that God designed the sexual union to be between one husband and one wife. All other expressions of sexual contact are outside His design and are not what is best for humanity. They are, as previously stated, an invitation to darkness in our lives. If we want to find balance in our marriages, and in all our other relationships, then following the principles of God as laid out in the Scripture is foundational.

UNDERSTANDING DIFFERENCES

There are many differences between male and female. Some are obvious and some are more subtle. When we think about the differences, we need to think of them in general terms. There are always exceptions to almost everything when there is DNA in the mix. Males and females are not like two atoms of Hydrogen and one atom of oxygen which makes one molecule of water. Hydrogen is always the same, it is not yellow then pink then brown. It is not large, small, then midsized. Neither is oxygen. Consequently, there is no generalization in oxygen or hydrogen, there is no bell curve of 'normal.' The diversity of humanity is because of the DNA that we carry, created by God. God loves diversity. Looking around at the creation, this becomes obvious. Even in some of the smallest of creatures there is diversity in the species. Yes, there are things that are the same about species, but there are also things that are different. All dogs have four legs, two eyes and two ears and one tail. We know a dog when we see one, but there are many shapes and sizes in dogs. We need to not get stuck on the exceptions here, but realize that there are generally things that are true for women and generally things that are true for men. Therefore, we will not use the word generalization from this point forward in the text, but the assumption of the generalization will be taken for granted.

MEN

Men are stronger physically, taller, and they have broader shoulders with more narrow hips. There are genitalia differences for men. Men are more apt to take risks, to do things that are dangerous or life threatening. Men are less articulate with language, less creative, have more of a focused mindset. Men struggle to express themselves emotionally. Men see the softer characteristics of humility, compassion, empathy, and mercy as weak, and signs of weakness in themselves and other men.

WOMEN

Women are less physically strong than men, shorter and have more broad hips. Women have mammary glands and different genitalia then men. Women are more creative, use both sides of their brains more easily, and have greater language skills. Women have a more multitasking mindset. Women can express themselves better emotionally and value the softer characteristics.

We may say that the culture is what has defined these characteristics in what we may term as 'gender differences' between male and female. There is an argument for 'cultural' gender distinctions. However, if you were to somehow be able to eliminate these 'cultural constructs' and have children grow up without them, the descriptions of the differences between male and female, listed above, would still be evident. There is more in the mix with the differences between female and male than culture. What we need to do is celebrate the God given distinctions rather than fight over them and so try to eliminate them. Women are different than men even if we only break it down to the simple biology of the physiological differences. Why is it so hard for us to recognize and celebrate the differences? Here is a truth that needs to be stated. Men and women are equal creations before God. In all the ways that matter, in the spirit realm, women and men are equal. *So in Christ Jesus you are all children of God through faith, There is neither Jew nor Gentile, neither slave nor free, nor is there male and female, for you are all one in Christ Jesus.* Galatian 3:27-28. This could be the reason why, in the heavenly realm, they are neither married nor given in marriage. (Matthew 22:30). If we could take away all the physicality of humanity and only see the spiritual, we would see that there is an equity that we miss in the physical realm. Therefore, women and men are equal before God.

While we are here in this physical realm, and we understand the differences between male and female, we can then recognize the God given design and purpose for why we are created as 'male and female.' While we function in this physical realm it is really important to see that God designed and ordained distinctions of female and male. These differences become distinct in the commands of God to marry and 'be fruitful and multiply.' Therefore, there are obvious differences in the roles for the family. Men cannot have children, that is a God given role of the woman and specifically the wife. Men are given the leadership role in the family. They are not superior, but they are appointed the head in the family by God.

When we consider that God created the husband and wife to be one, we should see some of the conflict in marriage resolved as the couple comes to understand that they are one in heart, one in purpose, one in spirit, one in body, one in soul and one united as parents for their children.

One of the issues for men is the abdication of their responsibility in the family. Men want to have a role like a stag with a herd of does. Solomon epitomized this mentality with close to a thousand wives and concubines. Hopefully, there is no need to delineate that illustration. However, God created us to be above the animal kingdom and to take dominion in the sense of stewardship over His creation. This mandate was not given to the man alone. Genesis 1:26-28: *26 Then God said, "Let Us make man in Our image, according to Our likeness; and let them rule over the fish of the sea and over the birds of the sky and over the cattle and over all the earth, and over every creeping thing that creeps on the earth." 27 God created man in His own image, in the image of God He created him; male and female He created them. 28 God blessed them; and God said to them, "Be fruitful and multiply, and fill the earth, and subdue it; and rule over the fish of the sea and over the birds of the sky and over every living thing that moves on the earth."*

The purposes of God were given to both husband and wife. They are to work together, and the husband is not to shirk his responsibility to lead. When the husband leads his family, as Christ leads the church, then it is much easier for the family to submit to that lead. Husbands should be Jesus to their wives, and wives should be the church to their husbands. Look at this classic passage of Scripture from this viewpoint. Ephesians 5:22-33: *22 Wives, be subject to your own husbands, as to the Lord. 23 For the husband is the head of the wife, as Christ also is the head of the church, He Himself being the Savior of the body. 24 But as the church is subject to Christ, so also the wives ought to be to their husbands in everything.25 Husbands, love your wives, just as Christ also loved the church and gave Himself up for her, 26 so that He might sanctify her, having cleansed her by the washing of water with the word, 27 that He might present to Himself the church in all her glory, having no spot or wrinkle or any such thing; but that she would be holy and blameless. 28 So husbands ought also to love their own wives as their own bodies. He who loves his own wife loves himself; 29 for no one ever hated his own flesh, but nourishes and cherishes it, just as Christ also does the church, 30 because we are members of His body. 31 For this reason a man shall leave his father and mother and shall be joined to his wife, and the two shall become one flesh. 32 This mystery is great; but I am speaking with reference to Christ and the church. 33 Nevertheless, each individual among you also is to love his own wife even as himself, and the wife must see to it that she respects her husband.*

Imagine a marriage that mirrors this passage of Scripture. The reason that the marriage relationship is presented as an illustration of Jesus and the church is because the marriage relationship is the relationship of complete oneness and intimacy. Too often, when inevitable conflicts arise in marriage, including female-male conflicts, they are not handled correctly or even in a Scriptural way. This leaves unresolved issues in the marriage relationship, and then bitterness begins to creep into the marriage. Couples can learn to understand and appreciate the differences between women and men. People can also learn to celebrate the differences between the sexes in all different types of relationships. When this is done there should also be less conflict between male and female in all types of relationships. Men should not expect women to act like men, and women should not expect men to act like women. God created us differently on purpose, and when we work together, correctly, understanding and celebrating the differences, there is a complimenting that happens. This complimentary relationship is not possible when there is adversity between the sexes.

When it comes to men leading, here is another interesting Scripture, Ephesians 6:4: 4 *Fathers, do not provoke your children to anger, but bring them up in the discipline and instruction of the Lord.* Do husbands leave this up to their wives? When we observe families, do we see this as an issue? Men should step into their God designed role in the family, and lead as God directs. One of the issues with this biblical principle is the nature of God's wisdom verses the wisdom of the world, or as James calls it, earthly, sensual wisdom. Sensual in the sense that this wisdom is more connected to base senses of humanity like taste, touch and what we feel. Philosophies like, 'If it feels good, do it.' This is not God's way. The kingdom of heaven is upside down compared to the kingdoms of this world. This is the reason why there is tension in the world and a need for balance. God says that weakness is strength, love your enemies, poor is rich and so forth.

All the wisdom from above, as James calls it, is counter-intuitive to the wisdom of this fallen world. This is why it seems so difficult for husbands and wives to follow the mandate of Ephesians 6. If there is a struggle with this in a marriage, and there usually is, then another struggle comes from the flawed thinking that the spouse needs to go first. She says she will respect him when he loves her, and he says he will love her when she respects him. God says that since the man is the leader, therefore, he should lead and that means he gets to go first. Husbands and wives can become complimentary in their shared leadership in the home. When there is a oneness that God intended between a wife and husband, then there is a sharing of leadership and responsibilities in the home under the servant leadership of the husband.

Can there be a balance between female and male, husband and wife? Yes! There can be a balance, but more than the fact that there can be a balance, there should be a Godly, respectful balance. We all need to show respect for each other and treat each other with the dignity and honor that is due an image-bearer of God Almighty.

I realize that this chapter has probably raised more questions than answers. Please read the Scripture and allow the Holy Spirit to teach. Please ask God for answers to your questions, and see what He has to say about Himself and His creation. This is the best way to understand truth.

CHAPTER TWELVE

Spirit and Flesh
The Balance of Our
Daily Walk

We waded into this subject in Chapter 10. Now we need to dive deeper into the balance of spirit and flesh. Balancing anything, and really everything, in the kingdom, is the result of us leaning into the leading of the Holy Spirit and learning to walk in the Spirit as Jesus did. As humans, we have a propensity for being out of balance. That does not have to be true for believers. We can live in the balance of life and our daily walk that God intended and live in abundance. Jesus promised us life in abundance. Is that what we see when we look at our lives? One of the greatest struggles of balance is the spirit and flesh. Jesus said that there is a struggle one with the other: *40 And He came to the disciples and found them sleeping, and said to Peter, "So, you men could not keep watch with Me for one hour? 41 Keep watching and praying that you may not enter into temptation; the spirit is willing, but the flesh is weak."* Matthew 26: 40-41. Paul said this is a struggle to the point that the flesh and the spirit are contrary or in opposition one to another: *16 But I say, walk by the Spirit, and you will not carry out the desire of the flesh. 17 For the flesh sets its desire against the Spirit, and the Spirit against the flesh; for these are in opposition to one another, so that you may not do the things that you please.* Galatians 5:16-17. Paul has a great treatise of this issue in Romans 7.

Although it is not added here, it is important that you read it and see how Paul describes the struggle between the flesh and the spirit. The spirit referenced here is our human spirit working in conjunction with the Spirit of God. We must be born again so our spirit has the life of the Holy Spirit. Ephesians 2 says that we were dead in our sin and being born again rectifies that deadness. However, when the spirit of humanity is made alive by the Spirit of God, the conflict with the flesh begins. This conflict constitutes an aspect of spiritual warfare.

When considering our salvation experience, what is interesting is that the things in the Old Testament, were written for our admonition. Paul gives the admonition of those who are in the period of the New Testament in Romans 15:4: *4 For whatever was written in earlier times was written for our instruction, so that through perseverance and the encouragement of the Scriptures we might have hope.* 1 Corinthians 10:1-11: Paul also says, *1 For I do not want you to be unaware, brethren, that our fathers were all under the cloud and all passed through the sea; 2 and all were baptized into Moses in the cloud and in the sea; 3 and all ate the same spiritual food; 4 and all drank the same spiritual drink, for they were drinking from a spiritual rock which followed them; and the rock was Christ. 5 Nevertheless, with most of them God was not well-pleased; for they were laid low in the wilderness. 6 Now these things happened as examples for us, so that we would not crave evil things as they also craved. 7 Do not be idolaters, as some of them were; as it is written, "The people sat down to eat and drink, and stood up to play." 8 Nor let us act immorally, as some of them did, and twenty-three thousand fell in one day. 9 Nor let us try the Lord, as some of them did, and were destroyed by the serpents. 10 Nor grumble, as some of them did, and were destroyed by the destroyer. 11* ***Now these things happened to them as an example, and they were written for our instruction, upon whom the ends of the ages have come.***

These passages are interesting because when you line them up with our salvation experience there is a matching of the two that is striking. Israel was in slavery in Egypt, we were in slavery to sin. Israel needed a miracle to be set free from Egypt. (They got more than one!) It was the miracle of Christ's birth, death, and resurrection that sets us free from sin. The Israelites were baptized in the sea. We are baptized in water. They had spiritual food and drink, and we have spiritual food and drink in the communion. When we get to the edge of the promised land and see the giants of sin in our life, do we then wander in the wilderness for forty years because the giants in our lives are too big for us to handle? That's what the Israelites did for forty years.

Paul encourages us here not to follow their example, but to trust God by the power of the Spirit within and overcome our giant sin issues. Do we as believers seemingly wander around lost in life because we chose not to deal with the 'giants in the land?' Not choosing to deal with our giants causes us to live a life of daily imbalance.

When I came to this understanding years after I was saved, I realized God had been leading me as a new believer to deal with the sin that was in my life. I should have trusted God back then because years later those sins had really taken root in my life. My biggest struggle was with my anger. When God led me to a place of serious refection and conviction, I realized that my sin was not only a giant in my life, but it was also an affront to the God I loved. I was so broken that I asked God to remove my sin of anger completely. The experience I had with God after that prayer felt like I had a huge hole in my chest, and I was having a hard time breathing. When I finally came back to a place of rest, God showed me that my anger was like a log inside me, and He had only taken a sliver of the log. The anger being completely taken, as I wanted and asked for, did not happen in that moment. God also showed me, from a book called, *Pursuing God,* by A.W. Tozer, that the sin of anger that I allowed in my life, and loved, defined me. He showed me that if He had taken it from me completely, like I had wanted, I would have physically died from the removal of the anger.

Around the same time, I was trying to live the life of a

believer, and I thought that going to church once a week was living that spiritual life. Getting my spiritual food weekly was what I thought I needed to do. It seemed to work for a while, but I realized, eventually, I needed a different lifestyle to truly live the life of a believer. I still went to church, but I added a daily reading and prayer time to my routine thinking that this would work, believing that it was a daily walk. This again worked for a while, and when it also did not satisfy, I then heard and read about walking in the Spirit. Jesus demonstrated it, Paul talks about it, but I did not know what it meant. I read and studied and eventually God convicted me that the spiritual walk of 'walking in the Spirit' was a moment-by-moment life with a more focused dependence on the Spirit.

One day, while I was still learning this principle, I was driving to work and worshipping God while listening to spiritual music in my truck. Suddenly, a person turned out in front of me, and I had to slam on my brakes to keep from having an accident! I was shaken and upset, and I said out loud, "You Idiot!!" As soon as the words were out of my mouth the Holy Spirit smote my heart, and I realized that I had sinned. Rather than try to justify my reaction, I humbled my heart, under conviction, and confessed my sin, and asked for forgiveness. I love that God is so forgiving. Immediately, I was able to 'be in the Spirit' again and return to worship and praise with the music. This incident drove home for me the moment-by-moment nature of believers walking in the Spirit. This was also the place where I realized that if I stayed in close relationship with the Spirit I could, in sincerity, go to God in prayer at any moment. This is what I believe Paul meant when he said to pray without ceasing. To be in a place of constant relationship so that going to prayer is like talking to a friend who walks with you everywhere.

Paul talks about the struggle of living spiritually, and when we read Romans 7, we can sympathize with Paul because the struggle is real. The flesh is weak in the sense that we give in to it too easily. But Paul also wrote: *I say then: Walk in the Spirit, and you shall not fulfill the lust of the flesh...the fruit of the Spirit is love, joy, peace, patience, kindness, goodness, faithfulness, 23 gentleness, self-control; against such things there is no law. 24 Now those who belong to Christ Jesus have crucified the flesh with its passions and desires. 25 If we live by the Spirit, let us also walk by the Spirit.* Galatians 5:22-25. Learning to walk 'in the Spirit' is the answer to walking a spiritual life of balance. God does not expect us to be perfect. He *does,* however, want us to trust Him. He *does* want a dynamic relationship of intimacy and passion with Him. He *does* want us to love Him above all other things in our lives. When we think about the 'demands' that God gives us do we secretly think that He is selfish when He asks these things of us? The reality is that when God asks, requires, or even commands these things it is not what is best for Him. These things that He requires are truly what is best for us. We cannot detract anything from God or add anything to

God.

Therefore, His pleasure in us following His commands comes because this is how our lives become blessed and a blessing to others. When we follow God as David mentions in Psalms 42: *As the deer pants for the water brooks, So pants my soul for You, O God. 2 My soul thirsts for God, for the living God,* it is *f*rom this place, like David, we can do as James tells us: *8 Draw near to God and He will draw near to you.* James 4:8. This nearness and closeness to God keeps us in a place of undivided fellowship and facilitates us walking in the Spirit.

The maturity to get to this spiritual place takes a fair amount of physical time. We often think we know what is best for us and do not remember that God really is working all things together for our good. God loves the maturation process. We see this in everything He has created. Everything starts from a seed and grows to maturity. Sometimes with adult believers the time is shortened because they possess a level of maturity when they become believers. We see this with the disciples/apostles. What happened during those three years with Jesus was that they learned to trust and follow Him and His leading. When He ascended, He promised to send the Spirit. The apostles moved from trusting and following the lead of Jesus, to trusting and following the lead of the Holy Spirit. Philip is a good example of following the lead of the Spirit. Acts 8 reads: *29 Then the Spirit said to Philip, "Go up and join this chariot." 30 Philip ran up and heard him reading*

Isaiah the prophet... 39 When they came up out of the water, the Spirit of the Lord snatched Philip away; and the eunuch no longer saw him but went on his way rejoicing. 40 But Philip found himself at Azotus. Is this what we see as normal spiritual activity? It should be and so should walking in and trusting the leading of the Holy Spirit.

Balancing our daily walk of spirit and flesh is possible when we learn to listen to the Holy Spirit, walk in the Spirit, and be obedient, like Philip, when He directs us. This balance is begun by our learning to discern the voice of the Holy Spirit within, and trusting His direction enough to follow that direction. Then we get to see all the amazing things that God wants to do through us as a manifestation of His glory here on earth.

Conclusion

Why is there a necessity for us to understand divine tension and apply balance? Because God has a very specific plan for each one of us. Though we each have our own destiny to walk, and that destiny is individualized for each of us, there is an overarching plan that God has in place for all of His children. Understanding balance helps us to cooperate with God in the overarching plan. We love Romans 8:28 because it gives us hope that all the things that happen to us are being worked by God in our eternal tapestry and, therefore, it is for our good. We often stop at verse 28 before we see why God works everything together for our good. Romans 8:28-30:

28 And we know that God causes all things to work together for good to those who love God, to those who are called according to His purpose. 29 For those whom He foreknew, He also predestined to become conformed to the image of His Son, so that He would be the firstborn among many brethren; 30 and these whom He predestined, He also called; and these whom He called, He also justified; and these whom He justified, He also glorified.

Paul says we are called, and then also gives us the expanded version that we are not *just* called. We have been predestined to be conformed to the image or likeness of His Son, Jesus. How do we become transformed from how He found us to the image and likeness of His Son? The same way that Jesus was 'transformed' into the vessel that God used to change the world. Suffering. We often think of the suffering Savior by remembering what He suffered during his trial and crucifixion. But the suffering of Jesus goes back to his very birth. The very stigmatism of the events around Jesus's birth caused suffering. Look at the Messianic Psalms 69:7-12:

7 For I endure scorn for your sake, and shame covers my face. 8 I am a foreigner to my own family, a stranger to my own mother's children; 9 for zeal for your house consumes me and the insults of those who insult you fall on me. 10 When I weep and fast, I must endure scorn; 11 when I put on sackcloth, people make sport of me. 12 Those who sit at the gate mock me, and I am the song of the drunkards.

Hebrews 5:7-8 says, *7 In the days of His flesh, He offered up both prayers and supplications with loud crying and tears to the One able to save Him from death, and He was heard because of His piety. 8 Although He was a Son, He learned obedience from the things which He suffered.*

We shrink back from suffering in our culture, but suffering is the way Jesus was made perfect. When we see and submit to the plan of God for our lives it becomes easier to walk a life of balance. A life of balance is rooted in trusting God. When Jesus was perfected by His suffering, His ministry changed the world. Imagine that all believers understood the work of the Father to bring us into the image of His Son. Imagine that they trust and submit to this perfecting work. Then imagine that all believers walk as Jesus walked while He was on this earth. If His three years of ministry changed the world, think what would be possible if millions of believers truly followed His example in the places that God had planted them. Is this possible? Yes! Living a life of balance is an integral part of being like Jesus.

Resources:

1. Lucas, Jim. What Is the Strong Force? *LiveScience*, Purch, 1 Nov. 2014, www.livescience.com/48575-strong-force.html.

2. Jackson, John Paul. True Spirituality. https://streamsministries.com/product/true-spirituality/.

3. Searle, John R., *Freedom and Neurobiology: Reflections on Free Will, Language, and Political Power*. Columbia University Press, 2008.

4. Wikipedia

5. *What Is It?*, Charles G. Finney: Power From On High - Christian Classics Ethereal Library, ccel.org/ccel/finney/power/power.iii.html.

6. Doctrine of KENOSIS., *Robert McLaughlin Bible Ministries*, gbible.org/doctrines-post/doctrine-of-kenosis/.

7. *The rise of the papacy by David Wells*. Ligonier Ministries. (n.d.). https://www.ligonier.org/learn/articles/rise-papacy

8. Ashcraft, J. (2021, June 15). *What did Jesus mean 'on this rock I will build my church'?* Christianity.com. https://www.christianity.com/wiki/church/what-did-jesus-mean-on-this-rock-i-will-build-my-church.html

9. *New Studio architecture*. New Studio Architecture. (n.d.). Retrieved November 28, 2022, from https://

www.newstudioarchitecture.com/

10. New Life School of Ministry. Jerusalem

11. Remember the Titians Movie., 2000. Walt Disney Pictures.

12. Greek word death, G2288. www.blueletterbible. org.

13. How Many Verses in the Bible Are About Money? https://blog.rose-publishing.com/?p=5465

14. Here's How Much the Average Person Makes in 30 Countries Around the World. https://www.gobankingrates.com/money/wealth/average-person-income-around-world/

15. Hebrew word side, H6763. www.blueletterbible. org.

16. https://www.chabad.org/parshah/article_cdo/aid/3085917/jewish/The-Creation-of-Man-and-Woman.htm.

17. https://www.thetorah.com/article/the-making-of-adam

18. https://www.psycom.net/oxytocin